engage

"Christians are weird!" Whether or not you agree with this
statement, the Bible clearly calls believers to be different.
All of the books we're following in this issue show us how
we can live radically different lives for God. We don't have to
be weird, but we do need to shine for Jesus in a dark world.

✱ DAILY READINGS Each day's
page throws you into the Bible, to
get you handling, questioning and
exploring God's message to you —
encouraging you to act on it and talk
to God more in prayer.

THIS ISSUE: Stand out from the
crowd with **Daniel;** discover real
Christianity in **1 John;** turn back
to God with **Ezra;** be challenged by
Proverbs; and track down Jesus'
true identity with **Mark.**

✱ TAKE IT FURTHER If you're
hungry for more at the end of an
engage page, turn to the **Take it
further** section to dig deeper.

✱ STUFF Articles on stuff relevant
to the lives of young Christians. This
issue we look at the **idols** in our lives.

✱ ESSENTIAL Articles on the
basics we really need to know about
God, the Bible and Christianity.
This issue, we get the lowdown on
baptism and communion.

✱ REAL LIVES True stories,
revealing God at work in people's
lives. This time we meet Helen, who
felt unloved, alone and worthless.

✱ TRICKY tackles those mind-
bendingly tricky questions that
confuse us all, as well as questions
our friends bombard us with.
This time we dicuss **euthanasia.**

✱ TOOLBOX is full of tools to help
you understand the Bible. This issue
we look at being a **copycat.**

**All of us who work on engage are
passionate to see the Bible at
work in people's lives. Do you
want God's word to have an
impact on your life? Then open
your Bible, and start on the first
engage study right now...**

HOW TO USE engage

1 Set a time you can read the Bible every day

2 Find a place where you can be quiet and think

3 Grab your Bible, pen and a notebook

4 Ask God to help you understand what you read

5 Read the day's verses with **engage**, taking time to think about it

6 Pray about what you've read

BIBLE STUFF
We use the NIV Bible version, so you might find it's the best one to use with **engage**. If the notes say **"Read Daniel 1 v 1–7"**, look up Daniel in the contents page at the front of your Bible. It'll tell you which page Daniel starts on. Find chapter 1 of Daniel, and then verse 1 of chapter 1 (the verse numbers are the tiny ones). Then start reading. Simple.

In this issue...

ENGAGE 18 IS BROUGHT TO YOU BY:

Weird writers: Martin Cole   Cassie Martin   Carl Laferton   Helen Thorne
Stand-out designer: Steve Devane
Unique proof-readers: Anne Woodcock   Nicole Carter
Slightly strange editor: Martin Cole (martin@thegoodbook.co.uk)

Daniel

Dare to be different

Do you ever feel pressure to fit in? Erm, stupid question, we all do! Whether it's something as harmless as your choice of footwear, or music to listen to, or whether to join in with under-age drinking, or drugs, or sex before marriage; we face peer-pressure all the time.

Now picture yourself in this situation: You're forcibly removed from your home, taken to a different country, given a new name, taught to speak a different language, sent to a foreign university and even given new gods to worship. Imagine the pressure to fit in!

That's exactly what happened to Daniel and his friends. Despite many warnings over hundreds of years, God's people (Israel) kept rejecting Him, so (as He'd warned them) they were sent away from the promised land. Enemy nations conquered Israel (the northern kingdom) and then Judah (the southern kingdom) and took God's people into exile.

Daniel was from Judah and was carried off to Babylon (present day Baghdad) where all of the above things happened to him. But despite being almost brainwashed by his new masters, Daniel was helped by God to stay faithful.

Your situation isn't very different from Daniel's. Your citizenship is in heaven (Philippians 3 v 20), but you're living in a hostile world that would love to brainwash you with its values and ideas. Let's immerse ourselves in this life-changing book and see what we can learn from the way God helped Daniel to be different.

1 Controlling interest

The beginning of Daniel is a national tragedy for God's people. Although God's people are taken away from God's promised land, God doesn't desert them. He's with them even in a hostile, foreign land...

👁 Read Daniel 1 v 1–7

ENGAGE YOUR BRAIN

▷ What happens to Jerusalem?

▷ Who is behind this attack? (v2)

▷ What is King Nebuchadnezzar's tactic for making his enemies part of his empire? (v3–5)

▷ Who did he pick? (v3–4)

Imagine having everything going for you and then being deported, taught a new language, given new food, a new boss, even new names.

▷ How likely is it that these Jewish exiles would stay true to God?

▷ Yet who is in control? (v2)

TALK IT OVER

Be honest. Do you ever catch yourself thinking: "Life would be so much easier if I wasn't a Christian"? Have you ever thought of yourself as an exile like Daniel and his friends? You're surrounded by people with different values and beliefs. How can you keep trusting God and depending on Him? Talk it over with a Christian friend, and share some ideas.

PRAY ABOUT IT

God was in charge. It wasn't just that He knew what was happening — He was actively encouraging it (v2). Even when we can't understand why things happen, we can hold on to the fact that God is in control.

Thank God that He's in control even when events look dire. Thank Him that He's able to keep you going as a Christian — ask Him to do that today.

THE BOTTOM LINE

God is in control.

→ TAKE IT FURTHER

Grab some more on page 107.

2 ┆ Food for thought

"Start as you mean to go on." Often your first actions have an impact on what follows. What will Daniel do? Will he stand up for God in enemy territory or will he worship their gods and enjoy the good life?

👁 **Read Daniel 1 v 8–21**

ENGAGE YOUR BRAIN
- ▶ What were the king's arrangements for Daniel and his friends? (Look back to v5.)
- ▶ What is Daniel's concern? (v8)

The food that came from the king's table probably included food that God had told His people not to eat as it was unclean (pork, shellfish etc) and it may also have been dedicated to the Babylonian gods — a double no-no.

- ▶ What does Daniel propose as an alternative? (v12)
- ▶ What happened? (v14–16)
- ▶ Why? (v9)

The consequences for the chief guard could have been bad if Daniel's proposal didn't go well (v10), but once again, God was in control.

- ▶ How does God bless Daniel and his friends? (v15, v17)

▶ Where do they end up? (v19)

It's not always easy to do things God's way. But when we trust Him in the little things, He builds our Christian character so we are able to also trust Him in the big things.

GET ON WITH IT
Is there something in your life that you know God wants you to do or stop doing? Will you obey Him in the little things today?

PRAY ABOUT IT
Ask for God's help to be like Jesus, who was obedient even to death (Philippians 2 v 8). Thank Him that because Jesus was obedient, we can be forgiven when we aren't.

THE BOTTOM LINE
Trust God in the little things; He won't let you down.

→ TAKE IT FURTHER
Feast some more on page 107.

5

3 | Nightmare situation

Dreams about flying mean you're gaining a new perspective, er, apparently. Let's face it, most dream interpretation is made up by the so-called interpreters. King Nebuchadnezzar was well aware of that.

👁 Read Daniel 2 v 1–9

ENGAGE YOUR BRAIN

▶ *Who does the king turn to? (v2)*

▶ *What does he promise them if they can/can't interpret his dream?*

▶ *What's the catch? (v9)*

That's clever. Any fool can make up a plausible interpretation for a dream they've heard about. But you'd have to have supernatural knowledge to know what the dream was without being told, in which case you must also know its true meaning.

👁 Read verses 10–23

▶ *Are the wise men of Babylon able to help the king? (v11)*

▶ *Who do they say is able to do what he asks? (v11)*

▶ *What is the king's response? (v12)*

▶ *How does Daniel react? (v14–18)*

Daniel is wise in how he handles the executioner, polite in his request to the king, and humble in seeking God's mercy and help. He's not just concerned for his and his friends' safety but also, the rest of Babylon's wise men.

▶ *How does God respond? (v19)*

▶ *Why is God the only one who can answer this request? (v20–23)*

PRAY ABOUT IT

Why not uses verses 20–23 to praise God now for who He is?

→ TAKE IT FURTHER

Follow the dream... to page 107.

4 | The interpreter

So the king's dream and its meaning were a mystery. But not to God. And now, not to Daniel. Imagine the suspense as, at the eleventh hour, before all the wise men face the chop, in comes Daniel with the interpretation.

👁 **Read Daniel 2 v 24–49**

ENGAGE YOUR BRAIN

▶ Who does Daniel say is responsible for interpreting the dream? (v27–28)

▶ Why is this so important?

▶ What was the dream about? (v37–45)

▶ How does God remind Neb who is the most powerful King of all?
v37:

v44:

v45:

Bible historians have matched up all these different kingdoms to the Mede and Persian, Greek, and Roman empires etc but the main point is that God is in control of history. He gave Nebuchadnezzar his power and He is in charge of the future too.

▶ How does Nebuchadnezzar respond to all this? (v46–48)

▶ What is Daniel and his friends' position at the end of this chapter?

▶ Who is in control of their lives?

PRAY ABOUT IT
In Matthew 28 v 18, Jesus says: "All authority in heaven and on earth has been given to me". Thank God now that Jesus is in control of our world and our destiny.

THE BOTTOM LINE
The LORD is the greatest King of all.

→ TAKE IT FURTHER
Meet the King on page 107.

5 | Feel the heat

More testing times for God's people in Babylon. This time it was Daniel's friends in the firing line. The heat is on.

👁 Read Daniel 3 v 1–15

ENGAGE YOUR BRAIN

▶ *Just how big is Nebuchadnezzar's ego?! (v1–7)*

▶ *Does it look as if he's learned anything about who the ultimate Ruler is? (2 v 47)*

▶ *How do Shadrach, Meshach and Abednego respond? (v12)*

▶ *What is the king's reaction?*

Nebuchadnezzar seems to have a little bit of an anger management problem. This is the second time we're told he flies into a rage, and if you remember chapter 1 v 10, it seems that his staff were constantly under the threat of execution!

👁 Read verses 16–30

▶ *What is Shadrach and co's brilliant answer? (v16–18)*

▶ *How does Neb take it? (v19–23)*

▶ *Why is it astonishing that these guys survive this furnace? (v22)*

▶ *Who is with them? (v25)*

God is with Shadrach, Meshach and Abednego. Right there, in the fire with them. It's a little foretaste of "Emmanuel" — one of Jesus' names — when God came to be with us and rescue us in person.

▶ *What does Nebuchadnezzar realise? (v26, v28–29)*

▶ *How does the chapter end? (v29–30) Any similarities to chapter 2?*

GET ON WITH IT

Do you need to stand up for what you believe in today? Is everyone around you worshipping other gods — money, popularity, appearance, relationships? God is with you. Ask Him to help you to worship Him only.

→ TAKE IT FURTHER

Turn up the heat on page 108.

6 ¦ God rules ¦

King Nebuchadnezzar is incredibly powerful and he has an ego to match. Remember the huge gold statue and the orders to worship him? With all that in mind, this letter from King Neb comes as quite a shock!

👁 Read Daniel 4 v 1–25

ENGAGE YOUR BRAIN

🔟 *What has Nebuchadnezzar come to realise? (v1–3) Surprising?*

🔟 *What prompted all this? (v5)*

🔟 *Who did he turn to? (v8)*

🔟 *What was his dream about? (v10–17)*

🔟 *What did it mean? (v22, 24–25)*

Nebuchadnezzar had everything going for him, but none of it was his own doing. In his pride he forgot that God is the true King.

👁 Read verses 26–37

🔟 *What is Daniel's advice to the king? (v26–27)*

🔟 *Does he take it? (v29–30)*

🔟 *How is Nebuchadnezzar restored to his position? (v34)*

🔟 *What does he realise? (v34–37)*

PRAY ABOUT IT

Are you tempted to pat yourself on the back for your achievements, good looks, popularity? How about your prayer life or Bible knowledge? Repent and remember that all things come from God (see Psalm 24 v 1 & Philippians 2 v 13).

SHARE IT

Were you surprised that someone like Nebuchadnezzar came to acknowledge God as his King? Is there anyone you know who you doubt could ever become a Christian? Why not talk to them about Jesus? God is the one who can change them!

THE BOTTOM LINE

God is the King, not you.

→ TAKE IT FURTHER

There's even more on page 108.

7 | God's graffiti

Have you heard the phrase "The writing's on the wall"? Well, this is where it comes from! We've moved on from the reign of Nebuchadnezzar to his son (or possibly grandson, the term "father" could mean ancestor), Belshazzar.

👁 Read Daniel 5 v 1–17

ENGAGE YOUR BRAIN

- ▶ What is Belshazzar's big mistake? (v2–3)
- ▶ How does he make it worse? (v4)
- ▶ What attitude does this show towards God?
- ▶ What is God's response? (v5)
- ▶ Who does the king look to for answers first? (v7)
- ▶ What does that tell us about him?
- ▶ Who does the queen suggest? (v10–12)
- ▶ How would you describe Daniel's attitude toward Belshazzar? (v17)

When you compare the way he spoke to Nebuchadnezzar, Daniel seems rude in his response to Belshazzar – "You can keep your rewards!" Maybe Daniel could see that Nebuchadnezzar would genuinely turn towards God whereas his descendant was arrogant and scared with no real desire to know the LORD.

👁 Read verses 18–31

- ▶ What does Daniel remind Belshazzar about Nebuchadnezzar? (v18–21)
- ▶ What does he point out about Belshazzar's behaviour? (v22–23)
- ▶ What is God's verdict? (v26–28, v30–31)
- ▶ Who does Belshazzar honour? (v29)
- ▶ Who should he have honoured?

Belshazzar said "No" to God and, tragically for him, God said "No" to him. God's word is final.

PRAY ABOUT IT

God graciously gives us time and opportunity to repent. Have you done this or are you still saying "No" to God? How about your friends and family? Spend some time now praying for God's mercy.

THE BOTTOM LINE

Are you listening to God?

→ TAKE IT FURTHER

Listen some more on page 108.

8 | Lion and cheating

Daniel in the lion's den is a great kids' story. But it's not just for kids and it's not really about lions. Just like yesterday's graffiti story, it's the tale of a human king meeting the heavenly King.

👁 Read Daniel 6 v 1–11

ENGAGE YOUR BRAIN

- ▶ *What position did Daniel hold in Darius' kingdom? (2–3)*

- ▶ *What was exceptional about him? (v4)*

- ▶ *What did his enemies do? (v5–9)*

- ▶ *Who were they really setting themselves up against?*

- ▶ *How did Daniel respond? (v10-11)*

Daniel might have been a big shot in Babylon, but his home was still Jerusalem and he still depended on God to help him in everything.

👁 Read verses 12–28

- ▶ *How is the king tricked? (v12–16)*

- ▶ *What does the king recognise about Daniel? (v20)*

- ▶ *And about God? (v20)*

- ▶ *How about after Daniel's miraculous rescue? (v26–27)*

Notice the lions aren't cuddled up with Daniel like the pictures in a children's Bible. These beasts were starving — God's angel had to shut their mouths! See what they do to Daniel's (and God's) enemies in v24!

PRAY ABOUT IT

What have these three kings (and you) learned about God in the last three chapters? Thank Him that He reigns eternally, that He is utterly in control, that He is powerful and that He cares for those who trust Him.

THE BOTTOM LIFE

God is the King who rescues.

→ TAKE IT FURTHER

Get your lion's share on page 108.

Idol worship

Name your idols. Maybe you're thinking of people you look up to and admire — a sports star or a singer. But what is an idol? When the Bible uses the word, it isn't thinking of the latest winner of a TV talent show!

STUPID STATUES

Idols feature loads in the Bible, even in the Ten Commandments, where God tells His people: "You shall not make for yourself an idol in the form of anything in heaven above or on the earth beneath or in the waters below. You shall not bow down to them or worship them; for I, the Lord your God, am a jealous God" (Exodus 20 v 4–5). So an idol is something that we worship instead of God.

In the Old Testament that mostly meant worshipping statues or idols made of metal, stone, wood etc. It should have been self evident that these home-made gods were a joke, but from the golden calf onwards (Exodus 32 v 1–4), God's people kept falling into the same old trap. Isaiah 44 v 9–20 is a blistering attack on how stupid the whole thing is. Check it out for a moment.

MODERN IDOLS

Ah, but we're OK, you may be thinking. Christians don't worship idols today. Some other religions or even other brands of "Christianity" might worship statues, but not us. We're far too sophisticated. Wrong.

The New Testament has some pretty harsh things to say about worshipping idols too. In Colossians 3 v 5, Paul urges the Christians in Colosse to get rid of all the things in their lives that were a problem for them before they became Christians. He doesn't just refer to physical idols but also to things like greed, which he calls idolatry. Just think about that for a minute.

Have you ever fantasised about winning the lottery? Be honest, who hasn't?! What would you spend the money on? That's idolatry right there. Sure, you might give some of it away, but what is your greedy heart really set on? It's an idol.

Think back again to that first definition of idolatry in Exodus 20. It's worshipping anything in God's place. So what do we put before God? Think of it the other way round. What would utterly destroy you if you lost it? Chances are it's an idol.

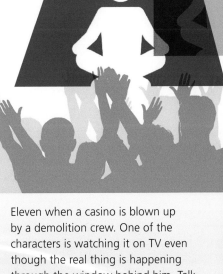

Your looks? Your brains? Your friends? Your family? Your boy/girlfriend? Your sporting ability? Musical talent? Even good things can become bad when they take God's rightful place at the centre of our lives. In fact they are the most dangerous kind of idol.

THE REAL THING

But there is hope. John writes at the end of his first letter: "Dear children, keep yourselves from idols" (1 John 5 v 21). But how do we do that? Look back to the previous verse: "We are in him who is true — even in his Son Jesus Christ. He is the true God and eternal life".

If we fix our eyes on Jesus Christ and see how wonderful, desirable and perfect the real thing is, we won't get misled by second-rate idols.

There's a moment in the film Ocean's Eleven when a casino is blown up by a demolition crew. One of the characters is watching it on TV even though the real thing is happening through the window behind him. Talk about missing the point! Similarly, no one would give their heart to an avatar when the real person is standing right next to them.

So it's no coincidence that the very first warning against idolatry in the Bible comes straight after an amazing declaration of who God is. Look up Exodus 20 v 2–3: "I am the Lord your God, who brought you out of Egypt, out of the land of slavery. You shall have no other gods before me."

This is the God who rescued us from far worse slavery than that found in Egypt (Hebrews 2 v 14–15). Why would we worship anyone or anything else?

1 John

Real Christianity

There seem to be so many different versions of Christianity out there that it's sometimes hard to know which is genuine. What is true Christianity and how can we be sure we're in touch with the real Jesus?

We need to listen to John. He wrote this letter so Christians can know for sure that they're following the real Jesus and heading for eternal life.

John was writing to a group of Christians who were being bamboozled by false teachers. These conmen had wormed their way into the church and their lies were tearing it apart from the inside. They claimed to be true Christians but they believed in a very different Jesus to the one we meet in the Gospels.

They didn't believe God's Son became human – they thought Jesus was just a man given the spirit of Christ for a while. In denying Jesus' true nature (as both man and God), they claimed His death achieved nothing. They also

seemed to think they were perfect and didn't sin. Or at least that their sin didn't matter.

Today, we still need to be on the lookout for false teaching as there are so many fake versions of Christianity. So many harmful ideas about Jesus that we must not be duped by. John points us back to the truth about Jesus and shows us how to spot spiritual conmen. Along the way, he builds up our faith and shows us how to truly live for Christ.

Got any doubts about your faith? Not entirely sure what real Christianity is? Or just want some encouragement in walking God's way? Then read on, asking God to speak to you powerfully through John's letter.

9 | Get the message

John's not one for wasting time with cuddly greetings. He's not even bothered about introducing himself. He wades straight in...

◉ Read 1 John 1 v 1–2

ENGAGE YOUR BRAIN

▷ What or who is John talking about?

▷ What does he repeat in each verse?

What an amazing opening to a letter! John gets straight to the point of what he's passionate about — "the Word of life". This is the message of Christianity which leads to eternal life. And it's also Jesus Himself. The Christian message **is** Jesus Christ. John and the other apostles saw Jesus in the flesh; they touched Him after He rose from the dead. See why we can trust what they tell us?

◉ Read verses 3–4

Wouldn't you expect John to say: "We're telling you about Jesus so you can be in touch with **Him**"?

▷ Instead, what does he say? (v3)

▷ Now read v3 again. Who is John in touch with?

So, if we want to be in touch with the true God and His Son Jesus (and that is the greatest human privilege), we need to be in touch with the true message of the apostles. Theirs is the true version of Christianity.

▷ What will the truth produce? (v4)

So, believing the right thing isn't just head knowledge. Our Christian joy depends on it.

PRAY ABOUT IT

Thank God for the true message of Christianity — Jesus Christ. Pray that you'll grasp what real Christianity is and meet the real Jesus as you read 1 John.

THE BOTTOM LINE

The message of Christianity is Jesus.

➔ TAKE IT FURTHER

Compare and contrast on page 108.

15

10 Travelling light

The spiritual conmen claimed to have special knowledge that put them right with God. But without Jesus in control of their lives, they were stumbling around in the dark.

👁 Read 1 John 1 v 5–7

ENGAGE YOUR BRAIN

🄳 How is God described? (v5)

🄳 How did the false teachers' lifestyle expose their lies? (v6)

🄳 What are the incredible promises for people who are in touch with God through Jesus? (v7)

Simple words, huge truth — God is light. That's total perfection. Flawless truth. All-revealing power. The false teachers claimed to be connected to God, yet the way they lived showed they were living a lie. Nothing we can do can put us right with God. Only Jesus' blood — His death on the cross — can make us pure, connect us to God and to other believers.

👁 Read verses 8–10

🄳 What did John say to people who claimed they didn't sin? (v8)

🄳 Yet what's the great news if we admit our sin to God? (v9)

The false teachers claimed that their immoral actions weren't really sinful! Not only were they deceiving themselves, they were going against God's teaching, calling Him a liar. God will have nothing to do with people who rely on themselves and turn their backs on Him.

THINK IT OVER

🄳 How will you "walk in the light" more?

🄳 How do you need to change your attitude to sin?

PRAY AND SHARE

Spend time confessing recent sins to God, who forgives everyone who trusts in His Son. Then turn v9 into your own prayer of praise.

→ TAKE IT FURTHER

Make light work of page 109.

11 | Sin solution

**Why is John banging on about sin in his letter?
All will be revealed right now...**

👁 **Read 1 John 2 v 1–2**

ENGAGE YOUR BRAIN

ⓘ *Why is John writing about sin? (v1)*

ⓘ *What's so brilliant about these verses?*

Christians still mess up and sin sometimes. But God has given us the ultimate solution to sin — Jesus Christ. He sacrificed His own life to atone for our sins — to make things right with God. If we trust in Him, Jesus comes to our defence. We've all sinned and deserve God's punishment, but Jesus is our defence lawyer — pointing to His own death in our place to rescue us from the death sentence.

👁 **Read verses 3–6**

ⓘ *What's a big sign that we know Jesus personally? (v3, 6)*

ⓘ *How did Jesus "walk"?*

God's love is made complete in Christians — they truly love God. And they show this by obeying Him, walking His way (v5–6). OK, we can't hope to live perfect lives as Jesus did. But we can live more and more for Him, changing, becoming more like Jesus, giving our lives to Him.

GET ON WITH IT

ⓘ *In what specific ways can you walk in Jesus' footsteps?*

ⓘ *How exactly do you need to obey Him more?*

PRAY ABOUT IT

Read through verses 1–6 again slowly, pausing after each verse to thank God, confess your sin or ask His help to obey Him.

THE BOTTOM LINE

Jesus is the solution to our sin problem. Walk His way.

→ **TAKE IT FURTHER**

Command central — page 109.

12 | Oh brother!

Love is mentioned in the Bible hundreds of times. It doesn't take a genius to work out that love is important to God. He loves us, He wants us to love Him, and He wants us to love other people too.

👁 Read 1 John 2 v 7–8

ENGAGE YOUR BRAIN

▶ *Was it a new idea that believers should love each other? (v7)*

▶ *So what's new about it? (v8)*

We all know Christians should love one another. It's old news — it's in the Old Testament. But it was also new — by His death on the cross, Jesus had shown how deep and amazing love should be.

👁 Read verses 9–11

The false teachers thought they were super spiritual and despised "ordinary" Christians. John says real Christians show love for their "brothers" — other believers. All Christians are God's children. We're brothers and sisters, so we need to show that deep, family love.

In the box, write the names of Christians you know. Include ones you like and ones you don't!

GET ON WITH IT

▶ *Do you show love to them?*
▶ *How?*
▶ *Who do you find it hard to be loving to?*
▶ *How can you show love and care for these people?*

PRAY ABOUT IT

Be honest with God about Christians you find it hard to love. Ask His help to be more loving to them. And make sure you do something about it.

➔ TAKE IT FURTHER

More from John on page 109.

13 | All-age worship

All Christians need encouragement and need to keep learning and growing. Today, John has important stuff to say to believers of all ages and all levels of growth and maturity. So listen up.

👁 Read 1 John 2 v 12–14

Here "children" are brand new Christians. "Young men" have been Christians longer and are growing in their faith. And "fathers" are believers who are mature in their faith.

New Christians

▶ What does John remind the "children" about?
v12:
v13:

If you're a new Christian, you've got loads to celebrate. You've had your sins forgiven and you're getting to know God Himself! Amazing. And if you're not yet a Christian — look what the Christian life has to offer!

Growing Christians

▶ How does John encourage these "young" believers? (v13, 14)

By His death and resurrection, Jesus has defeated the devil. By trusting Him, Christians are on the winning side too. So we should be bold and strong in our faith, letting God's word impact every aspect of our lives.

▶ Do you live like someone who has "overcome the evil one"?
▶ What needs to change?

Mature Christians

▶ What does John remind older Christians ("fathers") about?

The longer we've been Christians, the easier it is to take God's love for granted. We can forget how much He's done for us. But John says: Never forget this — you have a personal relationship with Jesus Christ, the eternal King of everything!"

PRAY ABOUT IT

If you're a Christian... you're sins have been forgiven by Jesus; you know God and talk to Him; you learn and grow from reading God's word; Jesus has already defeated the devil for you! You've got loads to thank God for, so what are you waiting for?

→ TAKE IT FURTHER

No *Take it further* today.

14 Worlds apart

John says one of the biggest threats to our faith is falling in love. Not the lovey-dovey, mushy stuff, but falling in love with the world.

👁 Read 1 John 2 v 15–17

ENGAGE YOUR BRAIN

▶ What's the warning if we love the world? (v15)

▶ What specific things are we warned against in v16?

▶ Why should we choose God over the world? (v17)

"The world" means human society in rebellion against God. It's so easy to fall for the world and all it has to offer — money, success, popularity, sex, career, family, having a good time. These things aren't wrong in themselves, but the world wants to trick us into living for them instead of God. To look for fulfilment in money, relationships or success, rather than finding it in Jesus.

👁 Read verse 16 again

THINK IT OVER

▶ What wrong stuff do you crave or chase after?

▶ Any problems with lust?

▶ How are you proud or boastful?

▶ What, with God's help, do you need to do about these things?

We must not fall for the lie that the world can bring us the satisfaction we crave. Or that we can make ourselves truly happy. Fulfilment, perfection and true happiness only come from Jesus. If we stick with God, we'll live for ever (v17) and one day live in true happiness and perfection with Him.

PRAY ABOUT IT

You know what you need to confess to God, ask Him for, and thank Him for today.

THE BOTTOM LINE

Don't fall for the world; live for God.

→ TAKE IT FURTHER

There's more on page 109.

15 | Antichrists

"You can't believe everything you read in the Bible."
"Jesus was a great teacher, but He wasn't God."
Sometimes it's hard to know how to reply when
people say stuff like that. John says: Stick to the truth.

👁 **Read 1 John 2 v 18–19**

ENGAGE YOUR BRAIN
▶ *What's John's warning?*

The last hour means the time between the first time Jesus was on earth and when He will return at the end of the world. We're in the last hour right now. The Bible warns us that people will teach us all kinds of lies. Sometimes the things they tell us sound so reasonable. But John calls them **antichrists** — they are against Jesus Christ and all He stands for.

👁 **Read verses 20–23**
▶ *What did the antichrists deny? (v22)*

▶ *Why does that matter?*

If anyone says Jesus isn't God or that He didn't die and come back to life, they're not believers. All Christians know the truth about Jesus and have been given the Holy Spirit to help them know what's really true (v20).

👁 **Read verses 24–27**
▶ *Why do John's readers need to say in touch with the message of the apostles? (v24)*

▶ *What happens to those who do stick with God? (v25)*

Christians have a great relationship with God the Father and with Jesus. God is with His people and has given them the Holy Spirit to help them out. Verse 27 doesn't mean we don't need other people to teach us about God. But it does mean we don't need any secret knowledge, as the conmen were claiming.

PRAY ABOUT IT
Thank God for giving you His Spirit to help you understand more about Him and to cling to the truth. Pray you'll never be fooled by lies about Jesus.

→ **TAKE IT FURTHER**
A little more help is on page 109.

16 | Family likeness

Imagine being in the royal family and all the privileges that would bring. OK, stop imagining, because Christians ARE in the royal family. Jesus is King and believers are part of His royal family.

👁 Read 1 John 2 v 28–29

ENGAGE YOUR BRAIN

ⅅ *Why should we stick with Jesus? (v28)*

Jesus will return. For now, we need to keep trusting in Him and living His way. Then we won't be ashamed when He returns, because we'll be confident that He has rescued us for eternal life with Him.

👁 Read 1 John 3 v 1–3

ⅅ *How do we know God loves us? (v1)*

ⅅ *When will the world see the truth about Christians? (v2)*

ⅅ *How does this great future affect how we live now? (v3)*

Incredible. All Christians are children of God! He lavishes His love on them. It's the greatest privilege in the universe. The spiritual conmen actually looked down on Christians.

But that's because they didn't know God and so didn't realise how special His people are. That will only become really obvious when Jesus returns and believers become like Him. We'll be like Jesus!

That doesn't mean we should wait to become more like Jesus. Through His Holy Spirit, He is transforming us to become more like Him, even before He returns and completes the job. We are God's children so we should start living like it. Purifying our lives (v3).

GET ON WITH IT

ⅅ *What part of life do you need to make more pure?*

PRAY ABOUT IT

Ask God's help to do it. Thank Him that He's changing you to be more like Jesus. And that one day all believers will be totally pure and perfect and like King Jesus!

➔ TAKE IT FURTHER

Like Father, like Son — page 110.

17 | Sin bin

Being good isn't easy. Even when we try to do what's right, we have wrong thoughts. Or we end up doing the thing we're trying so hard not to do. It's not surprising, really. There has only ever been one sinless person...

👁 Read 1 John 3 v 4–6

ENGAGE YOUR BRAIN

▶ Why did Jesus live on earth as a man? (v5)

▶ What difference should it make to our lives? (v6)

▶ What persistent sins do you need to stop?

👁 Read verses 7–10

▶ What other reason is given for Jesus coming into the world? (v8)

▶ Why don't Christians live the same way as everyone else? (v9)

▶ How can we tell the difference between God's children and the devil's? (v10)

The spiritual conmen thought God's moral laws didn't apply to them — they could do whatever they wanted. But they were dead wrong. Real Christians turn their backs on sin, striving to become more like Jesus, who was sinless.

Jesus' death and resurrection defeated the devil. One day, all the devil's evil work will be destroyed! Jesus hates sin and so should we. God's children still sin at times, but now they hate sin and fight against it, with the help of God's Holy Spirit.

THINK IT OVER

▶ Do people you see regularly know you're a Christian or do they think you're the same as everyone else?

PRAY ABOUT IT

Ask God to help you to really hate sin. Focus on one sin in your life and ask God to help you fight it.

THE BOTTOM LINE

Jesus has defeated sin, so kick it out of your life.

→ TAKE IT FURTHER

A few more thoughts on page 110.

18 ┆ Kids' talk

Time for a quick psalm — a song to God. This one's by King Solomon, David's son, who was given great wisdom by God. It's about, er, builders and arrows. Or maybe something a little deeper than that.

👁 Read Psalm 127 v 1–2

ENGAGE YOUR BRAIN

Notice the three parts: building (v1a), watching (v1b), working (v2).

▶ What two words are used in each part?

▶ Try completing this phrase: "You can build/watch/work all you like, but..."

▶ So how can we know whether our work is in vain or not?

Let's get the clues. Working all the hours you can to get money/status etc is stupid because you're forgetting:
a) you'll end up exhausted (v2);
b) God's in charge (v1);
c) all good things come from Him (v2)

The psalm's second half talks about one of God's gifts.

👁 Read verses 3–5

▶ How do these verses change your perspective on kids?

We can view children as a nuisance. But Solomon says they bring blessing, protection and strength. Kids are a gift from God — a "heritage" from Him (tell that to your mum/dad next time you're home late!).

THINK IT OVER

▶ How does this psalm teach us to be humble?

▶ What does it say about God's rule and our responsibility?

▶ What effect will this have on what you do and how you do it?

PRAY ABOUT IT

Think how this psalm teaches us to be grateful to God. What aspects of daily life will you now thank Him for?

→ TAKE IT FURTHER

Don't worry, go to page 110.

19 ┊ True faith

We often think of the Old Testament being full of doom, gloom and God's punishment. But here's another psalm that looks on the bright side.

⊙ Read Psalm 128

ENGAGE YOUR BRAIN

To be blessed is the life worth having — to be truly happy.

▶ *What two things mark out someone who is blessed? (v1)*

▶ *For those who lived this way, what could they expect?*
v2:
v3:

▶ *What's the prayer for such people? (v5–6)*

For God's Old Testament people who walked this way, the blessings from God were obvious — wealth, family, contentment. For us, the benefits that come our way as we show a right respect for God and obey Him are all to do with Jesus. In Him, we can know true peace and true prosperity as members of the true family of God. All our security, joy, riches and contentment can be found in Jesus.

And the promise for all believers is that one day we'll enjoy all of these things hugely and eternally.

PRAY ABOUT IT

Now sing or pray your psalm to God and talk about anything it has brought up.

Try rewriting this psalm in your own words, phrasing it for the present day Christian.

→ TAKE IT FURTHER

No *Take it further* today.

Baptism and communion

A MATTER OF LIFE AND DEATH

There's never been a more awesome event than Jesus' death and resurrection. He died to take the punishment we deserve for rebelling against God. He opened up the way to God. And He rose to life again, conquering death, so we can look forward to eternal life with God.

The trouble is, we're not very good at remembering important things about God. Having sinful hearts means that humans all too easily forget what's central and saving. To help us, Jesus left instructions for all Christians to do two things:

1. BAPTISM – STARTING WITH CHRIST

Jesus says that new Christians should be baptised (Matthew 28 v 18–20). That means publicly saying sorry for our sins and being washed with water (Acts 2 v 38). It might seem weird to get soggy in church but baptism is a great way to show, right at the start of your Christian life, that you're committed to relying on Jesus' death

and resurrection. In Romans 6 v 3–11, Paul says that being baptised is like being buried and rising again.

Death

When we're baptised, we remember that Jesus died to make us pure. And we remember that when we start following Jesus, our old life dies too — we stop living for ourselves and start living for God!

Life

We remember that Jesus rose again. And that we have the privilege of living in a brand new relationship with God as His Spirit makes His home inside us. We also have the wonder of eternal life to look forward to (Romans 6 v 22–23).

Over the centuries, Christians have disagreed massively over whether people should get baptised soon after they are born ("infant baptism" is a chance for parents to promise to bring up their children to know and follow Jesus) or when they are older

and decide to accept Jesus' invitation to follow Him for themselves ("believers' baptism"). If you don't know already, it would be great to find out what your church teaches about baptism. And if you're a Christian and haven't been baptised, it would be brilliant to find out how to take this exciting step.

2. COMMUNION – CONTINUING WITH CHRIST

Jesus also says we should regularly share bread and wine. This is called communion, the Lord's Supper or the Eucharist. Different churches do this in different ways but it always involves re-enacting the last meal that Jesus ate with His disciples (Luke 22 v 7–23). It reminds us that we need to keep relying on Jesus' death and resurrection.

On the night before He died, Jesus shared a meal that looked back on the Passover story of Exodus 12. At the first Passover, lambs were sacrificed so that the people of God could survive God's judgment and go to live in the promised land. Jesus tells His disciples that He is the ultimate Lamb of God, whose death allows all God's people to survive God's final judgment and live with Him for ever. It's another life and death reminder:

Death

As we take the bread (representing Jesus' broken body) and the wine (the blood He shed), we are reminded of His amazing sacrifice. And we show we think it's essential (1 Corinthians 11 v 23–26). This is something that only believers can do, so it's important that communion is only taken by people who are genuinely following Jesus (1 Corinthians 11 v 23 –29).

Life

We remind ourselves that we have been given new life as part of God's precious and united community (1 Corinthians 10 v 16–17). And as we eat and drink, we are strengthened for our Christian life and encouraged to rely humbly on Jesus' death and resurrection every day (John 6 v 53–58).

If you believe in Jesus' death and resurrection, why not talk to your youth leader or minister and ask about taking communion? It's a fantastic way to focus on the amazing life-and-death truths of the Christian faith until Jesus comes back again.

20 ┆ Daniel: Beast behaviour

Time for the second half of Daniel. It often gets missed out as it's, well, weird, and full of wild dreams and visions. But God uses Daniel's visions to teach us some incredible things about Him.

👁 Read Daniel 7 v 1–8

▶ *How would you describe Daniel's dream?*

▶ *Where do the winds come from?*

In the Bible, the "sea" is often code for the rebellious and chaotic world fighting against God. Despite the chaos below, notice that the winds come from heaven — God is still directing events.

▶ *These beasts represent different powerful kingdoms. How would you sum up the first three beasts/ kingdoms? (v3–6)*

▶ *But what suggests that these kingdoms are still under God's control? (v4–6)*

▶ *What is different about the fourth beast? (v7)*

This kingdom seems unstoppable. Do you ever look at the world, particularly certain parts of it, and worry that some evil is unstoppable? Perhaps when you see corrupt governments letting their people starve, or oppressive regimes torturing and executing their opponents? But take heart, as we've already seen, God is 100% in control.

PRAY ABOUT IT

Remember it's God's world! Why not spend some time now praying for His will to be done, "on earth as it is in heaven" — pray specifically for places or situations you know where people are rebelling against their Creator.

THE BOTTOM LINE

The world seems chaotic, but God is still the King.

→ TAKE IT FURTHER

Simply the beast — page 110.

21 | Throne zone

Daniel's wild vision continues. Don't worry — we'll get the interpretation of it next time, but for now, the action shifts to a courtroom.

👁 Read Daniel 7 v 9–14

ENGAGE YOUR BRAIN

▶ How is God described? (v9)

▶ What does this name tell us about Him?

▶ How is God described? And His throne? And his court? (v9–10)

▶ What does this remind us about Him?

▶ How does God treat the beasts? (v11–12)

God's judgment is absolute and totally just. He judges all humans, kings and regimes.

▶ How does that make you feel when you look at today's world rulers?

▶ Who else is present in the court? (v13)

▶ What does the Ancient of Days give to Him? (v14)

▶ How does the world respond to Him? (v14)

▶ What is His kingdom like? (v14)

Does that title "son of man" seem familiar? Yep, when Jesus chose it to refer to Himself, He was fully aware of this bit of Daniel!

▶ What does Daniel 7 v 13–14 remind us about Jesus?

PRAY ABOUT IT

Spend some time worshipping Jesus for who He was, is and will be eternally, using verses 13 and 14.

THE BOTTOM LINE

God's kingdom lasts for ever and Jesus is God's perfect King.

→ TAKE IT FURTHER

More on the son of man on p111.

22 | Victory insight

Daniel was freaked out by the first vision, so he asked one of the court officials to fill him in on the true meaning.

Read Daniel 7 v 15–28

ENGAGE YOUR BRAIN

▶ *What did the four beasts represent? (v17)*

▶ *But what's the great news for God's people? (v18)*

▶ *What is Daniel particularly concerned about? (v19–20)*

▶ *What will God's enemies do? (v23–25)*

▶ *But what will happen in the end? (v26)*

Saints = God's people: all of them, not just super holy folk with beards and sandals. If you're a Christian, you're a saint!

▶ *What is the great future for the people of God? (v27)*

▶ *But what will the short term involve? (v21, 25)*

Maybe that's why Daniel was so shaken by this vision (v28). Before God's ultimate victory and the wonderful future ahead of us, God's people will suffer. You only have to look around you to see this is true today.

PRAY ABOUT IT

Pray for Christians suffering around the world, that they would know the truth and comfort of v18, 22 and 27.

Check out http://www.opendoorsuk.org/pray/ for more prayer ideas.

THE BOTTOM LINE

God's people will suffer but they are on the winning side.

→ TAKE IT FURTHER

Further insight on page 111.

23 | Vicious attack

Another scary vision, two years later. Belshazzar is still king, so things are still really messed up.

👁 Read Daniel 8 v 1–14

ENGAGE YOUR BRAIN

- 🔹 Who is the first character that Daniel sees in his dream? (v3–4)
- 🔹 What is he like?
- 🔹 What is the next character like? (v5–8)
- 🔹 What happens to the ram?
- 🔹 Then who appears? (v9)
- 🔹 In what ways is this character powerful?

This all seems pretty weird so far, but the themes are the same as the last vision: power, conflict and victory. Notice, as before, that the target for all these powerful characters is God's people (v12).

- 🔹 What is the enemy doing in v11? (Prince of the host = God)

God's enemy goes straight for the temple, the place where God met His people. It's like those disaster movies where aliens blow up the White House — it's a symbol of the centre of power. Jesus' death was the ultimate sacrifice. So believers no longer need the temple and sacrifices — we can go straight to God. But Jesus' followers still have an enemy who wants to destroy them.

TALK IT OVER

Peter tells us that the devil "prowls around like a roaring lion looking for someone to devour". How can we stand firm in our faith? Read 1 Peter 5 v 8–9 and Ephesians 6 v 10–18 with another Christian, then chat and pray together about what you've read.

PRAY ABOUT IT

Ask God to keep you strong and safe in your faith.

THE BOTTOM LINE

Be on your guard.

→ TAKE IT FURTHER

Resisting the devil — page 111.

24 ┊ Vision explained

Daniel needed supernatural assistance to understand this vision (us too!), and so God sent his messenger, Gabriel, to explain it.

👁 **Read Daniel 8 v 15–27**

ENGAGE YOUR BRAIN

▶ What time period is Daniel's vision about? (v17, 19)
▶ Who do the ram and the goat refer to? (v20–21)

This "end time" starts with the Persian Empire, then Alexander the Great, and after that some more kings...

▶ What is the king in v23 like?
▶ How will he exert his influence? (v24)
▶ Just how big is his ego? (v25)

These verses are probably talking about a chap called Antiochus Epiphanes, who persecuted the Jewish people (v10) in Judah (v9) in 170BC. It's not hard to see who's behind him, though, is it?

▶ What time period is this vision also about? (v26)

Rebellion against God and persecution of His people is nothing new; it's a pattern that will continue until Jesus returns and puts a stop to it for ever. The devil was defeated at the cross but he is not yet destroyed.

▶ Why do you think Daniel was devastated by this vision and explanation?

PRAY ABOUT IT
Rebellion against God is ugly and we are all guilty of it. Say sorry to God for your own sin and thank Him for Jesus, who took the penalty for it. Pray for those who are still in angry rebellion against God, that He would have mercy on them and help them to see Jesus' rescue.

THE BOTTOM LINE
All rebellion against God is ugly and won't go unpunished.

→ **TAKE IT FURTHER**
More rebellious words on page 111.

25 ¦ Pray as you learn

Today's Daniel bit happened during King Darius' reign (he threw Dan into the lions' den). Remember, God's people are still exiles in Babylon and far from God's temple and the promised land.

👁 Read Daniel 9 v 1–3

ENGAGE YOUR BRAIN

▷ What gives Daniel new hope? (v2)

▷ Why could this be good news for Daniel and the rest of the exiles?

▷ What is Daniel's response? (v3)

The visions he'd had were pretty mind-blowing, but it's reading God's promises in His word that really gets Daniel excited. How about you?

👁 Read verses 4–16

▷ Why did Daniel think God might answer his prayer?
v4:
v7:
v9:

God's people had consistently rebelled against Him. That's why they'd been exiled in the first place, but since then they had still failed to turn back to Him and live His way. It didn't look as if God's promise to bring them home had any chance of coming true.

👁 Read verses 17–19

▷ What is Daniel most concerned about? (v17, 19)

▷ Why is this the only way to pray?

Daniel prays like Moses and other Bible greats — not on the basis of their own good deeds (or lack of...) but on the basis of what they know God is like — loving, righteous, merciful and forgiving. And Daniel wanted God to get the glory and honour He deserves.

PRAY ABOUT IT

When we come to God in prayer, it's only because of Jesus that we can call Him "Father" and know that He will hear our prayers. Spend some time doing that now, praying that God will get the glory He deserves.

→ TAKE IT FURTHER

Plenty more pertinent prayer pointers on page 111.

26 | Number cruncher

Dan prayed for Jerusalem to be restored, as God had promised. But there was more to understand about this promise. Cue Gabriel... who gives Dan a totally mind-boggling maths lesson.

👁 Read Daniel 9 v 20–24

ENGAGE YOUR BRAIN

▶ How quickly did the angel arrive? (v21, v23)

▶ How would Gabriel's words have encouraged Daniel? (v22–23)

▶ What God will do for His people and their city, Jerusalem? (v24)

▶ How long will it take? (v24)

God is going to act to put a stop to His people's sin, to restore their relationship with Him, to pay for their wrongdoing and make them "at one" with Him. He's also going to anoint — mark out as special — His holy one. Gabriel says this will take "seventy sevens" aka seventy weeks. But it's not literal — seven is the number of perfection in the Bible, so it's more like saying "in God's perfect timing".

👁 Read verses 25–27

▶ Who is on His way? (v25)

▶ What will happen to Him? (v26)

▶ What will he do? (v27)

▶ Who might this be talking about?

Daniel didn't see the full picture, but we do. Jesus has always been at the centre of God's plan to deal with His people's sin and bring them close to Him again. We might not follow all the details here but the big truth is awesome. Jesus saves.

PRAY ABOUT IT

Don't get bogged down in the detail — thank God for the eternal truth that Jesus came to deal with our rebellion and bring us back into relationship with our loving, all-powerful Creator.

→ TAKE IT FURTHER

More explanation of tricky v25–27 on page 112.

27 Shining example

Here's what's happening. King Cyrus has taken over from Darius and has let some of the Jews go back to Jerusalem (yay!) where they are rebuilding the walls and temple (double yay!); but they're also facing opposition (boo!).

👁 Read Daniel 10 v 1–6

ENGAGE YOUR BRAIN

▶ Just how upset is Daniel? (v2–3)

▶ Who does he see in his vision, and what is he like? (v5–6)

▶ Remind you of anyone? (Hint: Revelation 1 v 13–18.)

Our God is incredibly holy. Daniel's vision here and John's vision of Jesus show us a glimpse of how majestic, powerful, awesomely holy and, yes, totally terrifying He is.

👁 Read Daniel 10 v 7 – 11 v 1

▶ How does Daniel react in v8–10, and v15–17?

▶ What is it about God that makes him react like this?

▶ How did Daniel see himself in relation to God? (v17)

▶ What did God do to encourage him? (v18–19)

▶ Why did He do this for Daniel? (v12)

Life might look impossible, but God is awesomely powerful and in complete control. More than that, He cares for and strengthens His people.

PRAY ABOUT IT

"Peace! Be strong now; be strong," God says to Daniel (v19). Thank Him for His promise to you in Jesus: "In me you may have peace. In this world you will have trouble. But take heart! I have overcome the world" (John 16 v 33).

THE BOTTOM LINE

Jesus is our peace ad our strength.

→ TAKE IT FURTHER

More on today's tough verses on page 112.

35

28 War stories

Think about the last 100 years of your country's history. Imagine writing a quick summary of it without using any names of the key people involved. Confusing? You bet. Well, that's what this next part of Daniel is like.

👁 Read Daniel 11 v 2–35

ENGAGE YOUR BRAIN

▶ *What do these kings and military leaders have in common? (v3, v5, v11, v12, v14, v16, v21, v27, v28, v30, v32)*

•

•

•

▶ *Look at these characteristics. How are they like what we've seen in previous visions (and even in the kings of Babylon/Persia etc)?*

▶ *What is the outlook for God's people? (v30–35)*

Bible historians have suggested various matches for all these characters, but rather than getting bogged down in the detail, what is the big picture? Yep, arrogant human kings setting themselves against the heavenly King. Same old story.

▶ *Can you see this attitude in any countries or world leaders today?*

And just as God's people were persecuted here (v30–35), it's the same today. If we stand up for God, and tell people about Jesus, we will suffer. But it's a true privilege to serve God. Jesus went through far more pain and suffering for us, so that one day we will live with Him in perfect peace for ever, with no more suffering!

PRAY ABOUT IT

Read Psalm 2 and use it to shape your prayers today.

THE BOTTOM LINE

The LORD is King.

TAKE IT FURTHER

Put your armour on and run to page 112.

29 | Rise and fall

Daniel is learning about a future king who would become Public Enemy Number one for God's people.

👁 **Read Daniel 11 v 36–45**

▶ *What is this king's ruling philosophy (v36)?*

▶ *Is that usually a good way to live?*

If you think back to the book of Judges, you might remember the repeated line: "In those days Israel had no king; everyone did as he saw fit" (Judges 21 v 25). The result was total depravity and disaster. Left to our own devices, humanity has a nasty habit of making a mess of everything.

▶ *What will the outcome be for Israel (aka the Beautiful Land) and its inhabitants? (v41, v45, and look back to v31)*

▶ *What would eventually happen to this king? (v45)*

This king might be a nasty piece of work, but he's just being up front about what all human sin is — wanting to get rid of God and be God ourselves. Adam and Eve began it; we're all guilty of it.

PRAY ABOUT IT

Thank God for Jesus, "who, being in very nature God, did not consider equality with God something to be grasped, but made himself nothing, taking the very nature of a servant, being made in human likeness. And being found in appearance as a man, he humbled himself and became obedient to death — even death on a cross!" (Philippians 2 v 6–8)

THE BOTTOM LINE

We wrongly exalt ourselves, but Jesus humbled Himself...

➔ **TAKE IT FURTHER**

More about King Jesus — page 112.

30 The end?

A slow zoom out now for Daniel, past the immediate future, and the kingdoms to come, to the end of time and the only kingdom that will last for ever.

👁 **Read Daniel 12 v 1–4**

ENGAGE YOUR BRAIN

▶ *What must God's people expect before the end? (v1b)*

▶ *But what will God do for His people? (v1a)*

Michael is like a heavenly bodyguard, protecting God's people — they will always face opposition and hardship in this world, but...

▶ *What will God's people ultimately be delivered from? (v2)*

▶ *What will their future be? (v2–3)*

▶ *How about those people who set themselves up against God? (v2)*

A wonderful future — everlasting life and shining righteousness. Or everlasting shame and contempt. There's no middle way — you're either with God or against Him.

▶ *How will we know who God's true people are? (v1)*

Revelation 21 v 27 calls this book "the Lamb's book of life". It's Jesus' book and our eternal destiny is all down to how we respond to Jesus. Accept Him as Saviour and Lord or dismiss Him?

PRAY ABOUT IT

Talk to God now about people you know who reject, dismiss or ignore Him. Plead with Him to turn their lives around.

TALK IT OVER

Why is it good news that God will judge the earth? Chat it through with an older Christian.

TAKE IT FURTHER

Find some revelations on page 113.

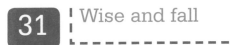

31 | Wise and fall

We've already seen what will happen when the world ends, but how will the book of Daniel end? By reminding him (and us) how to live in the meantime.

👁 Read Daniel 12 v 5–13

▷ *What are the two men discussing? (v5–7)*

▷ *Does Daniel get what's going on? (v8)*

▷ *What is he told to do? (v9, 13)*

▷ *What is the encouragement for him (and us if we're following Jesus) in v13?*

▷ *What are we reminded about life before Jesus returns? (v10)*

Don't take the numbers literally (v7, 11). They simply tell us that God's in charge. Not just of what happens, but when, too. The end will come at the time God chooses.

So how do we live now? Like Daniel, we must keep on following God. That's what it means to be wise (v10). It's wise to live your life in the light of what is to come. Even when it's unbearably hard, as Jesus warned us.

The end will come with the return of Jesus Christ. Daniel didn't know that. We do, from the New Testament. And God's prepared a great future for His followers. We get ready for it by following Jesus now.

PRAY ABOUT IT

Thank God for purifying you and making you spotless (v10) through Jesus' death and resurrection. Thank Him for refining you as you trust Him every day through the good times and the hard times. Pray for Him to have mercy on those who are currently rebelling against Him. Pray for specific people you think of.

THE BOTTOM LINE

There is a great future for those who follow Jesus.

→ TAKE IT FURTHER

One last thing from Daniel... page 113.

Unloved, alone and worthless?

Helen Thorne shares her powerful story.

A DIFFICULT CHILDHOOD

I guess I always thought God was real. But I never knew what He was like. My parents went to church when they were young but stopped when I was born. So I grew up in a home where there were lots of Bibles which were never read. And lots of opinions about church — but no real participation in it.

I was happy with that until I was about 7. But then life started to get harder. I developed a huge nose. And very mad teeth. And as a result I got badly bullied at school. I was pretty isolated and that made me easy prey for the local paedophile who lived down my street. Within a very short space of time I had moved from being a happy child to being someone who felt very unloved, very alone and totally worthless.

I reacted as many children react in such situations. By going completely off the rails. And by the time I'd reached my teens I was refusing to eat, cutting myself, overdosing regularly and drinking to excess. I was angry very angry with the people who had hurt me. And completely disillusioned with the God who wasn't stepping in to stop the pain. As far as I was concerned He either didn't care or wasn't in control.

ROCK BOTTOM

By the time I went off to university I'd hit rock bottom and ended up on a kind of rehab programme run by the counselling centre there. A Christian couple who I'd known for years supported me through that. And they made a massive impression on me. Whenever I screamed at them, they told me they loved me. Whenever I cut myself, they hugged me. Whenever I told them that God was horrible, they prayed. And after a while I became curious. I wanted to know how they could be so different, so radically loving.

So I agreed to go to church with them. There I started to hear about

God. Not some unknown God but a God who had revealed Himself in Jesus. For months I just listened and thought about Jesus' life, the cross and the resurrection and what it all means. And as I did so, He gradually started to change my heart. He helped me understand who He really is and how much He wants me to trust Him, follow Him and become more like Him…

AMAZING ACCEPTANCE

One day it all became clear. I wasn't unloved: I was adored by the creator of the universe. I wasn't alone: because of the cross, I could be washed clean and accepted into God's amazing family. And I wasn't worthless: I could be part of the most exciting thing in the world — I could follow Jesus and do His work. So I knelt down, said sorry for all the times I'd lived life my way instead of His and promised to follow Him as my King for the rest of my life.

It took a while to sort out all my issues with food, self-harm and drink. I still have to be quite careful now. And my nose is still huge and my teeth are still mad, so I continue to have to deal with people's hurtful comments from time to time. But things are massively different. By giving my life to Jesus I have gained so much — a loving King who is completely faithful. A wonderful new family of believers at church. And an amazing purpose in life that brings meaning to every moment of every day.

And I have the confidence that all this will last for eternity, and even get better! At the end of time, when Jesus comes back, I'm confident that, because He died for me, He will take me to live with Him for ever in a perfect place. He'll never reject me or send me away. He's the best King I could ever follow.

32 | 1 John: Real Christianity

After Daniel's mind-blowing visions, let's get back to John's great letter to believers. But be ready for more mind-blowing stuff as John shows us what real Christianity is.

👁 Read 1 John 3 v 11–15

ENGAGE YOUR BRAIN

- ▶ *What does John say real Christianity involves? (v11)*
- ▶ *What did Cain do? (v12)*
- ▶ *Why?*
- ▶ *What should Christians expect? (v13)*
- ▶ *What's a big sign that your life has been changed by Jesus? (v14)*
- ▶ *How serious is hatred? (v15)*

Real Christianity is full of love — even for people who hate us. Cain was jealous of his goody-two-shoes brother and murdered him (Genesis 4 v 1–12). John says if we hate anyone, we're as bad as murderous Cain!

THINK IT OVER

- ▶ *Who do you find it hard to love?*
- ▶ *Who do you treat badly and how?*
- ▶ *How will you change your hate-fuelled ways?*

Christians are not promised an easy ride. In fact, we're guaranteed to face opposition, even hate, from people who reject Christianity (v13). But we're expected to respond to this hatred with love! And also to show love to other believers (v14). A big sign that we love Jesus is that we show real love to other people.

Before you become a Christian, you're heading towards eternal death. But Jesus' death and resurrection rescues us and puts us on the road to eternal life. And the right response to this is to be truly loving to others.

PRAY ABOUT IT

Thank God for His immense love for you. Pray that you'll show His love to people, especially those you sometimes hate. Try praying about this every day this week.

THE BOTTOM LINE

The message is this: we should love one another.

TAKE IT FURTHER

Walk the hard road to page 113.

33 True love

How would you define true love in one sentence? Give it a try:

Read 1 John 3 v 16–18

ENGAGE YOUR BRAIN

▷ What was the ultimate example of love? (v16)
▷ So what is expected of us? (v16)
▷ What does that mean in practice? (v17)
▷ How is true love shown? (v18)

Jesus loves us so much that He died on the cross for us, so we don't have to take the punishment for our sins. Jesus gave His life for you and me! That's real love.

Love is costly. It means giving your life for others. Giving them your time, money, possessions, talents. Loving others means being less selfish. Giving up what you have to help and please other people. Words aren't enough. It's no good saying you love others but doing nothing about it!

GET ON WITH IT

▷ Who do you know who's in need?

▷ What can you give them or do for them?
▷ What "treasured possessions" will you share with people?

Read verses 19–20

Showing love for others is a sign that you're a Christian. Ok, we won't love everyone all the time. But if you're better at being loving and caring than you used to be, it's a good sign!

God knows us better than anyone. Even though He knows all our sins, He still loves and accepts us! If you've trusted Jesus to forgive your sins, then God accepts you as His child! And that doesn't change, even though we still mess up.

PRAY ABOUT IT

Read through today's verses again, talking to God as you do so.

→ TAKE IT FURTHER

Unbeatable love on page 113.

34 Confident Christianity

Yesterday we discovered that true love is being like Jesus — giving your life for others. Showing love for people is a sign that you really are a Christian, rescued by Jesus. Loving others boosts Christians' confidence.

Read 1 John 3 v 21–24

ENGAGE YOUR BRAIN

- ▷ What benefit does Christian confidence bring? (v21–22)
- ▷ What does God expect of His people? (end of v22)
- ▷ So what does that look like? (v23)
- ▷ What's true for people who live God's way? (v24)
- ▷ How do we know God is with us? (v24)

If you've trusted Jesus' death on your behalf, then you're a Christian — don't doubt it — you're saved! Have confidence. Start living like someone who's been rescued. Talk to God — He will answer your prayers! Trust in Jesus! Live God's way! Show love — real love — for the people around you! If you've been rescued by Jesus, live like it!

TRUST!

- ▷ Do you believe in Jesus and what He's done for you?
- ▷ So how does it affect your life?

PRAY!

- ▷ How is your faith in Jesus shown by the way you pray?
- ▷ How could your prayer life be different?

LOVE!

- ▷ Done any of the stuff you decided to do over the last 2 days?
- ▷ What's stopping you?

We try to live for God more and more because we love Him. We have a close relationship with Him. So close that God's Spirit lives in all believers, transforming them and helping them to do all of these things.

PRAY ABOUT IT

Only you know what you need to talk to God about today.

TAKE IT FURTHER

Confidently stroll over to page 114.

35 | That's the spirit!

The Christians John was writing to were being tricked by false teachers who were convincing them of lies about Jesus. Yet spiritual forces were behind these conmen and their lies.

👁 Read 1 John 4 v 1–6

ENGAGE YOUR BRAIN

▷ What did John advise his friends? (v1)

▷ What is the "Jesus test" he suggests? (v2)

▷ What's an obvious mark of false teaching? (v3)

▷ Why shouldn't we be scared? (v4)

False teachers claim that Jesus was not sent by God. They refuse to acknowledge that He was God's Son, who lived as a man on earth. They claim to be super spiritual and have secret knowledge. But if anyone tells you that Jesus isn't God's Son or He didn't become human or can't forgive sins... don't listen to them. They're not from God or even on His side.

GET ON WITH IT

▷ Know anyone who makes wrong claims about Jesus?

▷ What will you do next time you hear such lies?

👁 Read verse 4 again

We shouldn't worry too much about evil spirits. God is far more powerful than them. And Jesus has already defeated the devil. Christians are on the winning team!

PRAY ABOUT IT

Pray that you'll be able to spot the difference between true and false teaching. And that you'll hold on to the real Jesus.

THE BOTTOM LINE

Teaching that's really from God acknowledges Jesus as God's King.

TAKE IT FURTHER

Spirited stuff on page 114.

45

36 | Love letter

Yep, John's talking about love again. So why is it such a big part of his letter? And why is love at the heart of the Christian message? Well, love is at the very heart of God.

👁 Read 1 John 4 v 7–10

ENGAGE YOUR BRAIN
▷ What instruction does John give yet again? (v7)

▷ What reason does he give? (v7)

▷ How did God publicly show His love for us? (v9)

▷ What makes this love so astonishing? (v10)

Christians are God's children. Love comes from God. In fact, God **is** love — everything about God is marked by love. So we should seek to show that love to everyone we meet.

Look how powerful is the love God showed for us. He gave us new life at great cost to Himself. So our new lives should be filled with love. It should pour out of us, just as it pours out of God.

👁 Read verses 11–12

▷ So why should we love other believers? (v11)

▷ What's brilliantly true for all Christians? (v12)

The only response to the immense love shown by Jesus' death for us, must be to show love to everyone. One way God shows His love for people is through Christians. We can show God's love to people around us. No one has seen God, but people can see what God is like when we show real love to them! And He's given us the Holy Spirit to help us do this.

GET ON WITH IT
▷ What exactly do you need to do differently this week?

PRAY ABOUT IT
Read through today's verses, praising God and asking Him to help you show His love to others.

→ TAKE IT FURTHER
No *Take it further* today. Sorry!

37 ┆ Am I really a Christian? ┆

I know my friend Bob follows Manchester United because he wears the shirt and scarf, goes to their matches, and never stops talking about them. But how do you know if you're really a Christian? A follower of Jesus?

👁 **Read 1 John 4 v 13–16**

ENGAGE YOUR BRAIN

▷ *What four pieces of evidence help us to know we're Christians?*
v13:
v14:
v15:
v16:

👁 **Read verses 16–18**

▷ *Why is it dumb to claim to know God if we don't love others? (v16)*

▷ *What happens to people who love like God? (v17)*

▷ *Why will people who love have nothing to be scared of on God's final judgment day? (v18)*

👁 **Read verses 19–21**

▷ *Why should we love other believers?*

God wants us to know we are His — that He lives in us and we in Him. But how can we be sure? Well...

a) God's given us His Spirit (v13). So when we feel compelled to love others unselfishly, that's the Holy Spirit at work in us.

b) We've got the apostles' eye-witness reports to rely on (v14).

c) We've put our trust in God's Son, Jesus (v15).

d) We rely on and experience God's love (v16–18).

e) We love our fellow Christians (v19–21). God's love (v10) shows that's about actions, not just feelings.

PRAY ABOUT IT

If you have any doubts about whether you're really a Christian, take them to God right now. Ask Him to make it clear to you. Pray about any of the things you struggle with or worry about. And make sure you talk to an older Christian about it too.

→ **TAKE IT FURTHER**

Without a doubt, it's time to turn to page 114.

38 | Faith lift

John doesn't want Christians to have an inferiority complex. In chapter 5 he slaps down reasons for Christians to be encouraged.

👁 Read 1 John 5 v 1–2

ENGAGE YOUR BRAIN

▶ What's true for everyone who trusts in Jesus? (v1)

▶ What's the sign that we really love other Christians? (v2)

Be encouraged! All believers are now God's children, part of His family. You can tell who's part of the family because they show love for other Christians, they clearly love God and they obey Him.

👁 Read verses 3–5

▶ Why should we happily obey God and not moan about it? (v3–4)

At times it can seem impossible to keep going as a Christian. So many temptations, so much opposition. But everyone who trusts in Jesus can overcome sin and the influences of this world. Faith in Jesus acts like a shield against sin. We trust that He's forgiven us for our sin, so we want help to obey Him and fight sin. We'll still fail at times, but God will help us to sin less and less and to obey Him more and more.

PRAY ABOUT IT

Let's spend longer praying today. First, thank God that He helps us overcome sin! Now write down things you need Him to help you fight against.

Now ask Him. And keep asking Him all week.

➔ TAKE IT FURTHER

You've gotta have faith... page 115.

39 | Son rise

People were claiming that Jesus wasn't really God's Son. So John wanted to convince his readers of the truth about Jesus.

👁 Read 1 John 5 v 6–8

ENGAGE YOUR BRAIN

▶ What three pieces of evidence does John give that Jesus really is God's Son?
1. W
2. B
3. The S

1. Water

This is referring to Jesus' baptism. When Jesus was baptised, God said: "This is my Son, whom I love" (Matthew 3 v 16–17). Clear evidence that Jesus is God's Son!

2. Blood

Jesus bled when He died on the cross. He died to rescue us from our sins. Only God's Son could do that.

3. The Spirit

All Christians have the Holy Spirit with them. The Spirit helps them to know the truth about Jesus and to have faith in Jesus, the Son of God.

👁 Read verses 9–12

▶ What does God give anyone who accepts the truth about His Son? (v11–12)

▶ What about those who reject the truth?

Have you got your head around this? Everyone who believes the truth about Jesus and lives with Him as King of their lives... will share in eternal life with Him. The opposite is true for those who reject Jesus.

PRAY ABOUT IT

How has today's Bible bit encouraged you and challenged you? Let it affect and inform what you pray today.

THE BOTTOM LINE

He who has the Son has life; he who does not have the Son of God does not have life.

→ TAKE IT FURTHER

Deconfusication on page 115.

40 | Life assurance

John's letter. Nearly finished. But not yet.
More encouragement. And a confidence boost.
Plus: stuff about anger. And sin.

👁 Read 1 John 5 v 13–15

ENGAGE YOUR BRAIN

▶ Why did John write this letter? (v13)

▶ What else can Christians be confident about? (v14–15)

John wanted to tell Christians that Jesus really did die and come back to life so their sins could be forgiven. Many of these Christians were doubting their faith and John wanted them to be sure they were Christians.

"If we ask anything according to his will, he hears us." We know what God's will is — what pleases Him — by reading the Bible. And asking Him to show us. If we pray for things that please God, He'll hear our prayers and answer.

👁 Read verses 16–17

▶ What's one thing we can pray about?

The "sin that that leads to death" probably means totally refusing to believe in Jesus. Like the false teachers, who John's been warning us about. People who reject Jesus will be punished. But other sins can be forgiven! If a Christian friend is struggling with sin, ask God to help them. Pray for them over and over.

PRAY ABOUT IT

Thank God that He hears our prayers and answers them. Think of at least two Christian friends/relatives. Ask God to help them loads in their fight against sin. And pray that God will give you more confidence in what you believe.

→ TAKE IT FURTHER

Check out Jesus' prayer tips on p115.

41 | We know, we know, we know

It's time for John to sign off. But before he does, he gives us a few important reminders.

 Read 1 John 5 v 18–21

ENGAGE YOUR BRAIN

▷ *What three things do we know? (Put them in your own words)*
v18:

v19:

v20:

▷ *And what final instruction does John give? (v21)*

Verse 18 isn't saying that Christians never sin. But they now live for God and not just to please themselves. They fight sin rather than enjoying sin. And Jesus ("the one ... born of God") helps Christians in their struggle against sin. Amazing.

After all, Christians are God's children (v19)! Yet most people in the world don't live God's way, so we have to be on guard not to be influenced by the world and fall into temptation. And Jesus will help us. He gives us understanding and a close, everlasting relationship with Him (v20). So it's dumb when we value things more highly than Jesus and put them first in our lives (v21).

GET ON WITH IT

▷ *What sin do you need Jesus' help to fight this week?*

▷ *How can you avoid the temptations around you?*

▷ *What "idols" do you need to get rid of?*

PRAY ABOUT IT

Thank God for the close relationship Christians have with Jesus. Thank Him that He will keep them safe. Pray that you'll put what you've learned today, and throughout 1 John, into practice.

→ TAKE IT FURTHER

We know there's more on page 115.

42 Psalms: Bittersweet songs

Time for a couple more songs to God. Today's psalm was written for God's Old Testament people — the Israelites — to sing. It looks back on hard times and is hard to swallow, yet contains a sweet truth at its centre.

👁 Read Psalm 129 v 1–4

ENGAGE YOUR BRAIN

▶ *As the psalm writer looks back, what negatives does he mention? (v1–3)*

▶ *And what great positives? (v2, 4)*

👁 Read verses 5–8

▶ *What does he pray for the enemies of God's people?*

The Israelites had been attacked and oppressed many times. They were even conquered and taken into exile. Yet God was in control, rescuing them and giving them many victories (v2, 4). Life had been painful for God's people but they could still trust in the Lord.

In the second half of this psalm, the writer turns on his enemies. It seems harsh, but he's praying that God would deal fairly with anyone who opposes His people ("Zion"). Yes, we're to show love and forgiveness to people who stand against us. But it's also right to ask God for justice (NOT revenge!). We're not to be judges ourselves though; only God is the perfect Judge.

PRAY ABOUT IT

Take extra time to pray today. Talk to God about hard times you've gone through. Thank Him for bringing you safely through them. Especially thank Him for sending Jesus to rescue you from your biggest enemy — sin. And pray about some of the terrible things going on in the world — whatever's on your mind. Ask God to bring justice to those situations.

THE BOTTOM LINE

The Lord is righteous; He has cut me free from the cords of the wicked.

→ TAKE IT FURTHER

The focus switches to Jesus on page 116.

43 | Pswedish psalm pstudy

We're going to try something different today. We'll look at this psalm using the "Swedish Bible Study Method". It's really simple and you can use it when you read any Bible bit, to help you get to the heart of God's word.

👁 **Read Psalm 130**

ENGAGE YOUR BRAIN

After you've read the psalm carefully, write down what you've learned under each of these 3 headings.

1. Lightbulb
Something that "shines" to you from the verses.

2. Question mark
Something you don't understand or a question you'd like to ask the writer or the Lord.

3. Arrow
Something that jabs at your conscience or something you know you should do.

PRAY ABOUT IT

Now read through the psalm again. And then read what you've written down and talk about it all with God.

➔ **TAKE IT FURTHER**

Find a little more on page 116.

1

2

3

Ezra

Going home

**God's people are in a mess. They'd
split into two kingdoms, and both
repeatedly disobeyed God despite
everything He'd done for them.
But God wouldn't ignore their
descent into sin and they were
punished. First, Assyria invaded
the northern kingdom, Israel, in
722BC. Then, Babylon trashed the
southern lot, Judah, in 586BC, and
carried off many of God's people
to exile (in what is now Iraq).**

things get back to normal, with
God's people ignoring Him and doing
whatever they pleased?

**Ezra was given the job of turning
God's people back to Him. We'll
see if he did. In the process, we'll
learn more about God, more
about His work, more about His
plans and purposes. And more
about what it means for God's
people today (Christians) to live
as God's people.**

So, Ezra's book opens with God's
people suffering under foreign rule,
miles from home. Things were looking
bad. God had promised to bring His
people back. But there had been no
sign of God doing anything.

The story of what God did next is
phenomenal — He took His people
back to Jerusalem. But once there,
a big task lay ahead: rebuilding the
temple, city walls, houses, everything.
And would God's people get back
to living God's way and being a
distinctive people for God? Or would

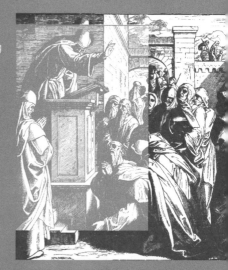

44 Time to go home

God's people were in exile in Babylon. And then superpower Persia took over, so King Cyrus was now in charge. But would things change for the better or worse under Cyrus?

👁 Read Ezra 1 v 1–4

ENGAGE YOUR BRAIN

▷ *How powerful was Cyrus? (v2)*

▷ *What was his surprising announcement? (v3)*

▷ *And what unexpected bonus did he throw in? (v4)*

▷ *Why did all this happen? (v1)*

Persia was the most powerful kingdom of the time. So Cyrus was like World President. Yet God used this mighty, egotistical, unpredictable dictator to achieve God's purposes and bring His people back to His city, Jerusalem.

👁 Read verses 5–11

▷ *Who got ready to return? (v5)*

▷ *How were they surprisingly helped by the locals? (v6)*

▷ *How did God show more of his faithfulness? (v7–11)*

God was rescuing His enslaved people again. It's a new, second Exodus! This time, though, it's a small group which goes. And their big concern is to serve God with a real devotion. God even ensured the temple treasure was safely taken back. It would come in handy later (chapter 3).

God was moving history in line with His plans. God was keeping His word to bring His people home. He always does what He's promised. And that's not only true on an international level, but in our small corner too.

PRAY ABOUT IT

Thank God that He's in control of history. He's the true ruler of the world. Pray that He will use the super-powers of the world in His plans. And ask Him to use your tiny life in His perfect plans too.

→ TAKE IT FURTHER

Time to go to page 116.

45 | The guest list

Yay! A long list of names and numbers! OK, so this chapter doesn't look extremely exciting at first glance. Yet in it we'll see God's great love and care, and we'll see His people's enthusiasm.

👁 Skim read Ezra 2 v 1–63

ENGAGE YOUR BRAIN

▶ *Who is listed in this chapter? (v1)*

▶ *What was the problem for some priests? (v61–62)*

▶ *What happened to them? (v62–63)*

This list is exciting! This is what was left of God's true people. The remnant that remained after the harsh pruning process of the previous years. These guys stood firm. If you were on the list, you were part of God's chosen people.

👁 Read verses verses 64–70

▶ *How many people returned to Jerusalem?*

▶ *What did some of them do? (v68–69)*

▶ *What's the situation at the end of chapter 2? (v70)*

What a turnaround! God's people had rejected Him and disobeyed Him over and over. So He punished them, allowing foreign armies to conquer them and take them away from the promised land. But the Lord had promised to save a small remnant and take them back home. And now it was happening! God was keeping His promise, and His people enthusiastically returned to His city.

THINK IT OVER

▶ *How have you seen God keeping His promises?*

▶ *In what ways can you be more enthusiastic in serving Him?*

PRAY ABOUT IT

Praise God for being completely dependable. Pray that you'll trust Him more and enthusiastically do what He asks you to do in life.

→ TAKE IT FURTHER

No *Take it further* today.

46 Altar-ations

The Israelites are back in Jerusalem. They could take it easy, just enjoying being back home. But God has brought them back and they want to show their gratitude.

👁 Read Ezra 3 v 1–6

ENGAGE YOUR BRAIN

- ▶ *After 3 months back home, what did they do? (v1)*

- ▶ *What did they decide to do? (v2)*

- ▶ *What worried them? (v3)*

- ▶ *What else did they do? (v4–6)*

- ▶ *What guided their decisions? (v2)*

- ▶ *What hadn't they done yet? (v6)*

God's people were back in God's city and they wanted to live His way. They carefully followed the laws God gave to Moses; they built an altar so they could offer sacrifices to God. They boldly built the altar to worship God, even though it might provoke the idol-worshipping people who lived near Jerusalem to attack them.

They also made sure they celebrated God's feasts. The Feast of Tabernacles re-enacted the journey from Egypt by living in temporary shelters. It reminded them that the great blessings they now enjoyed were only because God had rescued them from Egypt. We can be so settled and so used to all the great things we have that we forget that God provided it all.

THINK IT OVER

- ▶ *Anything you know God wants you to do that you're not doing?*

- ▶ *How can you show your thanks for all He's given you?*

PRAY ABOUT IT

Talk to God honestly about those two questions.

→ TAKE IT FURTHER

Sacrifice stuff is on page 116.

47 Apply some foundation

The Israelites are back in Jerusalem — and they're back to worshipping God, obeying His law and celebrating His feasts. But something's missing from Jerusalem. Time to get the trowels out...

👁 Read Ezra 3 v 7–13

ENGAGE YOUR BRAIN

- ▷ What was the big building project? (v8)

- ▷ What accompanied the foundation–laying? (v10)

- ▷ What did the people recognise about God? (v11)

- ▷ What were the different reactions to the temple rebuild? (v12–13)

The temple in Jerusalem was a hugely important place. It was the house of God; the place where God chose to share His presence with His people. It was the focus of their relationship with God.

So starting to rebuild God's temple was a moment of great emotion. It was the old guys who remembered the previous temple and wept loudly. Maybe because they remembered seeing it be destroyed. Or because

they knew this new one wouldn't be as great. But there were shouts of joy too — the excitement and anticipation of God being among His people again.

We don't need a temple or priests these days. When Jesus died on the cross, the temple curtain was ripped apart. There is no longer a barrier between us and God. Through Jesus, we can go straight to God.

PRAY ABOUT IT
Use v11 to kickstart your prayers today, praising God and thanking Him for His love — seen perfectly in Jesus.

→ TAKE IT FURTHER
Firm foundations found on page 117.

48 | The plot thickens

Ever get enthusiastic about something new happening at church or gospel-spreading opportunities? And then just when things are going well, everything goes wrong or you meet opposition and ridicule?

👁 Read Ezra 4 v 1–5

ENGAGE YOUR BRAIN
- ▶ What was the cunning plan of the Israelites' enemies? (v2)
- ▶ What was smart about Zerubbabel's reply? (v3)
- ▶ What happened next? (v4–5)

Discouragement, fear, frustration; this conflict persisted for most of the next century. Now slip some brackets around v6–23, and **read v24**. The building programme crashed for 16 years. Until... wait for chapter 5. Meanwhile, we're told about aggr that happened years later...

👁 Read verses 6–16
- ▶ What tactics did these guys use?
  v6–8:
  v13:
  v16:

👁 Read verses 17–24
- ▶ What did the king do?
  v19–20:
  v21:

- ▶ What was the depressing outcome? (v23–24)

The sad truth is that there are people in the world who will stop at nothing to oppose God's people and God's plans. The Christian life will not be easy and we definitely *will* face opposition. Sometimes it will be subtle (eg: friends slowly leading us away from God). And sometimes it will be blatant and upsetting (eg: lies being spread about us). But remember this — God's plans can't be stopped. As we'll discover tomorrow...

PRAY ABOUT IT
Spend plenty of time praying for every Christian you know who's facing persecution or opposition. Ask God to stop the plans of His enemies and to strengthen His people as they make a stand for Him.

→ TAKE IT FURTHER
More opposition on page 117.

49 | Work in progress

God's people were back in Jerusalem. They were full of enthusiasm and started to rebuild the temple. But their enemies succeeding in stopping the project. Building work on God's house ceased for over 10 years.

👁 Read Ezra 5 v 1–5

ENGAGE YOUR BRAIN

- ▶ Why did they decide to start building again? (v1–2)
- ▶ What problem surfaced? (v3–4)
- ▶ Why had God's people no real reason to be scared? (v5)

👁 Read verses 6–17

- ▶ What was Tattenai concerned about? (v8–10)
- ▶ What brilliant reasons did the Israelites give for the building project? (v11, v13–16)
- ▶ What was Tattenai's fair request? (v17)

👁 Read Ezra 6 v 1–12

- ▶ What did they discover? (v1–5)
- ▶ What was sensational about King Darius' orders? (v6–12)

What a turnaround! God's people were disheartened and gave up on rebuilding the temple for years. So God sent prophets (messengers) to fire them up into starting again, which they did. Amazingly, King Darius got behind them, stopping opposition (v6, 11), paying expenses (v8) and providing sacrifices for God (v9–10)! Amazing.

We *will* face hard times living as Christians and doing God's work. But don't assume that will always be the case or use it as an excuse for chickening out. Support can come from the most surprising places, like this powerful, idol-worshipping king. God's plans cannot be stopped, so expect the unexpected.

PRAY ABOUT IT

Talk to God about any "hard" gospel work you're involved in or know of. Maybe a local mission, a Christian meeting at school/college or even just telling your friends about Jesus. Ask God to make that work successful in whatever way He wishes. And be prepared for surprising results.

→ TAKE IT FURTHER

Who's Haggai? Try page 117.

50 Celebration nation

Shocker. Powerful Persian king, Darius, has commanded his officials to help the Israelites with rebuilding God's temple in Jerusalem. So God's people got building.

👁 Read Ezra 6 v 13–18

ENGAGE YOUR BRAIN

▶ What finally happened? (v15)

▶ Who had supported the project? (v14)

▶ How did the people celebrate?
v16:
v17:
v18:

It was God who moved Cyrus to set God's exiled people free. It was God who got them rebuilding the temple. It was God who changed Darius' heart to let them continue. And after a 16-year delay, God's temple was completed. God's plans will always work out. And that's true even when we can't see how it will happen.

👁 Read verses 19–22

▶ What else did the Israelites celebrate? (v19)

▶ Why? (v22)

The Israelites turned back to God. They saw how God had taken them back to His city, how He'd protected them, and how He'd changed Darius' mind. They had loads to be thankful for, so they thanked God. Loads.

SHARE IT

What can you look back on and thank God for? Why not grab some Christian friends to spend time together, looking back on what God's done for you, thanking Him and celebrating it. A positive praise party.

PRAY ABOUT IT

Hopefully, you've got loads to thank God for. So you know what to do right now.

→ TAKE IT FURTHER

More from Haggai on page 118.

51 | Ezra's entrance

Noticed anything strange about the book of Ezra?
There's been no mention of anyone called Ezra! Well,
that's about to change. Around 60 years after God's
temple was completed, Ezra made an appearance.

👁 Read Ezra 7 v 1–10

ENGAGE YOUR BRAIN

▶ Why should God's people listen
to Ezra?
v1–5:
v6, 10:

▶ Why were things going well for
Ezra? (v6, 9)

Read verses 11–28

▶ What did the king give to Ezra
to take to Jerusalem?

▶ What was Ezra's job? (v14, 25)

▶ What would happen to anyone
who disobeyed God's laws? (v26)

▶ When Ezra spoke, what did he
recognise? (v27–28)

▶ So what was he able to do? (v28)

We need to listen to the people
God has chosen to teach us from
the Bible. Show them respect. Listen
to them. Check that what they're
saying is what the Bible says. If it
is, obey it. Apply it to your life. The
consequences are dire for anyone
who rejects God's teaching.

GET ON WITH IT

▶ How can you listen better to Bible
teachers?

▶ How can you make sure you do
what God teaches you?

Ezra recognised that God was in
control. Things were only going well
for Ezra and Jerusalem because God
was lovingly looking after them and
doing incredible things for them.

PRAY ABOUT IT

Done anything good recently?
Will you take the credit or do you
recognise who's behind it? If so,
thank Him now and make sure He
gets the credit He deserves.

➔ TAKE IT FURTHER

Fill in the time gaps on page 118.

52 | Ezra's exodus

When Ezra embarked on the 4-month journey from Babylon to Jerusalem, he took several thousand more of God's people with Him. So they could live in God's city too.

👁 Skim read Ezra 8 v 1–14

Yay! Another list of names! This one details who accompanied Ezra on the latest exodus back to Jerusalem. The Lord was continuing to protect His people and keep His promises.

Read verses 15–20

▶ Who was missing? (v15)

▶ How did God deal with the problem? (v18–20)

Levites were temple servants. We don't know exactly why having no Levites around was so bad or why no Levites travelled with Ezra back to Jerusalem. But we do know that God sorted the problem and even raised up a useful new leader (v18).

Read verses 21–23

▶ What did Ezra do and why? (v21)

▶ Why did this group have no bodyguards? (v22)

▶ What was better than bodyguards? (v23)

THINK IT OVER

▶ What should we do when we're worried?

▶ What are you worried about?

▶ So what will you do right now?

PRAY ABOUT IT

Let's copy Ezra as we pray today.

1. He fasted. Take time out from stuff you'd normally do to spend extra time talking to God.
2. He was humble. Admit your sins & failings to God. Ditch that ego!
3. He asked. Tell God what's on your mind and ask Him to help you.
4. He noticed. Make sure you notice when God answers your prayers. Think back to stuff you've prayed about. How has God answered?

→ TAKE IT FURTHER

Missing verses found on page 118.

53 ┊ Wedding yells

Ezra was an expert on God's law. He was sent to Jerusalem to get God's people to follow God's law again. To really live as God's people. But he was in for a shock.

👁 Read Ezra 9 v 1–4

ENGAGE YOUR BRAIN

▶ *What was the scandal? (v1)*

▶ *What made it even worse? (v2)*

▶ *What did this show about the people's attitude to God?*

God expected His people to be different to other nations and to be loyal to Him. But they inter-married and so tolerated other gods and evil behaviour.

👁 Read verses 5–15

▶ *What did Ezra say was the result of the people's sin? (v7)*

▶ *Yet how had God treated them? (v8–9)*

▶ *How did the people respond to God's great love? (v10–11)*

▶ *What did God have the right to do? (v13–14)*

God's people continued to disobey Him. He'd given them far more than they deserved. And what was their response? The way they lived showed a chronic lack of respect for God. An unwillingness to live His way. Marrying outsiders meant disobeying God and accepting their gods. Being influenced by people who hated God. The Lord expects undivided loyalty and worship from His people.

THINK IT OVER

▶ *How have you seen God's love for you?*

▶ *And how have you responded?*

PRAY ABOUT IT

Thank God for being so loving and merciful to you despite your sin. Thank Him for sending His only Son to show how much He loves you. Pray about other "gods" and bad influences you need to get rid of.

→ TAKE IT FURTHER

More about marriage on page 118.

54 | Conscience challenged

Ezra's not happy. Despite the Lord protecting His people and returning them to Jerusalem, they've treated His laws lightly. So what will they do about it?

👁 **Read Ezra 10 v 1–8**

ENGAGE YOUR BRAIN

▶ How seriously did Ezra treat sin? (v1)

▶ Who else took sin seriously? (v1)

▶ What was Shecaniah's positive spin on the situation? (v2–4)

Ezra was devastated by the people's disobedience. But he didn't angrily whip them into action. Instead, he pricked their conscience until they urged *him* to act. The people realised they'd let God down and were desperate to put things right.

THINK IT OVER

▶ What has God pricked your conscience about lately?

▶ How have you responded?

▶ What will you do now?

👁 **Read verses 9–17**

▶ What must they do? (v11)

▶ How did they deal with all the many cases? (v16–17)

The people had disobeyed God, and become so close to God's enemies, it took 3 months to sort it all out! Verses 18–44 detail exactly who had disobeyed God's marriage laws. The solution was painful but essential — those who'd married godless wives had to break from them and send them away.

Ezra called for **distinctive** lives for God. Compromising our behaviour displeases God, dilutes our faith and wrecks our witness.

PRAY ABOUT IT

Thank God for everything He's taught you through Ezra. Read the *Think it over* questions again and spend time praying about them.

→ **TAKE IT FURTHER**

No *Take it further* today.

55 | Soul song

Time to grab another psalm. This one's by King David and it's really short. So read it through twice. Out loud. Try to emphasise different words when you read it the second time.

👁 **Read Psalm 131. Twice.**

ENGAGE YOUR BRAIN

▷ How would you describe David's attitude towards God?

▷ What does he recognise? (v1)

▷ What do you think he means by "great matters" and "things too wonderful for me"?

▷ What has he learned to do? (v2)

▷ Can you explain his great plea? (v3)

▷ What do you like about this psalm?

THINK IT OVER

▷ Can you echo David's words in v1, honestly?

▷ What's your attitude when you come to read the Bible?

▷ What matters in life must you leave in God's hands, remembering He's in charge?

▷ Are you learning to stop and listen to God's word?

▷ In what ways do you need to trust Him more?

PRAY ABOUT IT

There's time today for you to come before God, admit what you've learned here, ask for a change of attitude, and resolve to keep relying on Him, day by day in the future. Why not read the psalm again, and take this opportunity?

➔ **TAKE IT FURTHER**

Question time on page 118.

56 | Back to the future

A psalm that takes us back into the depths of Israel's history — and forward to some great truths about Jesus. Come and take in a big picture.

👁 Read Psalm 132 v 1–10

Ark? Resting-place? Footstools? Priests? What's going on? Well, it's looking back to the time King David decided to build a "house" for God — in it would be kept the ark (containing the Ten Commandments), which symbolised God's presence with His people.

▶ *What motivated David? (v3–5)*

▶ *What's the great prayer? (v8–9)*

👁 Read verses 11–18

▶ *David had been talking about building a house, but how did God answer him? (v11–12)*

Look at the strength of God's commitment (v11). He won't revoke (cancel) this promise.

▶ *And what else did God promise? (v13–14)*

▶ *What would follow from this? (v15–16)*

▶ *What do v17–18 add to v11–12?*

Tricky Old Testament language here, but do you get the big idea? God promised...

• that He would dwell among His people.

• that He'd care for their daily needs.

• that He'd bring forgiveness to His people through sacrifice.

• that one from David's family would rule for ever.

See how it points to Jesus?

PRAY ABOUT IT

Thank God for His commitment to His promises, shown so fully and clearly in the work of Jesus.

→ TAKE IT FURTHER

Fast forward to the past on page 119.

67

A matter of life and death

Each issue in TRICKY, we tackle those mind-bendingly difficult questions that confuse us all, as well as questions that friends bombard us with to catch us off guard.
This time we ask: What does the Bible say about euthanasia?

THE VALUE OF LIFE

Euthanasia is defined as the act of putting to death painlessly (or allowing to die by withholding medical treatment) a person or animal suffering from an incurable or painful disease or condition. Most of us would put a beloved pet "to sleep" or "out of its misery" and the argument goes that surely we should do the same for human beings? But are human lives really only as valuable as animal ones?

What makes a human life valuable? If you only had a certain amount of money to spend on cancer medicines would you give them to an 87-year-old man or a 30-year-old mum of three? Does a severely disabled child who will never be independent, and whose care will cost the taxpayer thousands, have the right to be born?

What about the young man who is completely paralysed and unable to speak, surely his life is not worth living? Shouldn't he be allowed the right to die?

All these questions come down to what it is that makes human life valuable. Is it our relationships? Our abilities? Our health? What we can contribute to society?

The problem is if we look in these places to find our value, we can soon be convinced that actually we're not valuable at all. Who has never felt useless, hopeless or a failure? At times, all of us will have nothing to offer and will need to depend on others. Does that make our lives worthless? Either all human lives are valuable or none are.

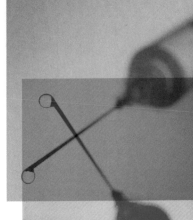

MADE BY GOD

Read Psalm 139 and think about what it tells us about God and about us (v1–4, v7–10 and v13–16). The Bible says we're valuable because God made us. We're His wonderful piece of craftsmanship, which means our lives have purpose and meaning. It's all dependent on our relationship with the God who made us, not our individual achievements (or lack of them).

A sculpture by Leonardo da Vinci is priceless, not because of itself — it's just a lump of rock that's been attacked with a chisel — but because of who created it. Every human life is valuable because it is the work of the Master.

SAVED BY JESUS

More than this, every human life is valuable because Jesus Christ shed His precious blood to redeem us. Jesus died for us, not because of anything we had done or could possibly contribute, but because He loved us (Titus 3 v 5).

Christians have the highest view of the value of human life, because they know that our lives belong to God, not us. If your neighbour lends you his car for a drive, you'll be a lot more careful with it than your own car. Our lives do not belong to us but to God. That means it is up to Him, not us, when He decides to end them. As Job put it when he faced the terrible loss of his children: "The Lord gave and the Lord has taken away; may the name of the Lord be praised" (Job 1 v 21).

That's not to say that some of the situations that people find themselves in (like the ones mentioned earlier) are not extremely hard. But every life is precious, and God promises to transform even our worst suffering into glory, just as He did with Jesus, if we put our trust in Him (Romans 8 v 16–18).

57 Proverbs: Walking God's way

The book of Proverbs is a collection of short, snappy sayings that will challenge you and the way you live. This is wisdom straight from God. If you want to take God seriously and live His way, Proverbs is the book for you.

Read Proverbs 10 v 1–10

ENGAGE YOUR BRAIN
▷ What's the link between all these verses?

OK, that was a trick question. There isn't a link. Yes, some of the proverbs cover similar topics, but there's no real thread or story linking proverbs together. We're going to read Proverbs in quite big chunks — so there's no way you'll be able to take to heart every proverb in a chapter. In fact, it's fine if you concentrate on just one proverb each day that really hits you.

▷ In what ways is the second line of each proverb related to the first?

▷ Which of these sayings do you find surprising?

▷ Which is most interesting to you?

▷ Which one (or two or three) do you think God is using to speak specifically to you?

▷ What is He saying to you?

▷ What will you do about it?

PRAY ABOUT IT
Ask God to speak to you and teach you as we read Proverbs. Pray that He'll make it obvious which sayings to focus on each day. Ask the Lord to help you act on what you learn so that you grow closer to Him and live more for Him.

→ TAKE IT FURTHER
Walk on over to page 119.

58 | Shut your mouth!

Words are powerful. They can encourage and build someone up, or they can knock someone down and tear them apart. There are loads of proverbs about what comes out of our mouths. What we say is vitally important.

👁 **Read Proverbs 10 v 11–21**

ENGAGE YOUR BRAIN

▶ How can we use words in very different ways? (v11)

▶ How have you been like v18 recently?

▶ Who do you need to say sorry to?

▶ So how can you avoid upsetting people with sinful words? (v19)

▶ How can you use words positively? (v20)

▶ Who do you need to build up and "nourish"?

▶ How exactly will you do that?

Shut your mouth! Are you surprised that the Bible tells us to shut up? Well it does. When we talk too much, it's more likely we will say something we shouldn't — lies, gossip, slander, causing division. So shut up. Don't talk so much. That way you'll actually think about what you say and make sure it's worth saying. Ask yourself: is what I'm saying nourishing or is it hurtful or ungodly?

GET ON WITH IT

▶ Who do you often upset with your choice of words?

▶ How can you honour God more in your conversation with them?

▶ What kinds of things do you talk about that maybe you shouldn't?

▶ So what will you do?

PRAY ABOUT IT

You know what you need to say to God today. Choose your words carefully.

→ **TAKE IT FURTHER**

More choice words on page 119.

59 Good vs evil

More wise words from Proverbs. Today we'll try to learn something from each verse. As you read them, note down which proverbs really speak to you and your current situation.

Read Proverbs 10 v 22–32

ENGAGE YOUR BRAIN

▶ What's the promise of v22?

▶ Does that mean all Christians will be rich?

▶ What are we told about people who refuse to live God's way?
v23:
v24:
v25:
v27:
v28:
v29:

▶ And what about those who obey God?
v23:
v24:
v25:
v27:
v28:
v29:

▶ What is v26 saying about lazy people ("sluggards")?

▶ What else are we told about words? (v31–32)

Is verse 22 really saying that God blesses His people with wealth? Well yes, but not necessarily right now. The New Testament doesn't guarantee wealth for Christians now, but it does guarantee heaven. All believers will be rich when they live with God for eternity. So this verse (and many others in Proverbs, look out for them) must be grasped with an eternal perspective.

THINK IT OVER

▶ What have you learned today?

▶ Which proverb is most relevant to your life?

PRAY ABOUT IT

Talk to God about your answers to those questions.

→ TAKE IT FURTHER

Grab some more on page 119.

60 Rich or righteous?

We've already seen that loads of the proverbs are about what we say. And loads are about the consequences of living for or against God. Well, loads more are about money and our attitude towards it.

👁 Read Proverbs 11 v 1–6

ENGAGE YOUR BRAIN

▶ Which of these six verses strikes you most?

Solomon seems to be saying a concern for right living is a better guide for life than a concern for wealth. Of course, it's easy for him to say that — Solomon oozed wealth. But you're probably feeling poor. So it's time to take the wealth test. Score one point for each "Yes" answer.

WEALTH TEST!

▶ Do you normally have at least one cooked meal a day?
▶ Does the place you live in have solid walls and a roof?
▶ Does your family own a car?
▶ Does your house have electricity and running water?
▶ Do you usually have at least one holiday a year?
▶ Does your government offer you free school education?

▶ Do you have a TV and/or your own phone?

How did you score?
0–2: How do you afford Engage?
3–4: You're richer than almost everyone Sol was writing for.
5–7: By world standards, you're rich. Even if you don't feel it.
8–10: Cheat. Tried the stock market?

👁 Read verses 7–17

▶ Is God speaking to you through any of these sayings?
▶ If so, what's He saying?

PRAY ABOUT IT

Thank God that Christians are truly rich — because of Jesus, believers have real treasure and an amazing future to look forward to.

→ TAKE IT FURTHER

Find true wealth on page 120.

61 | Rich pickings

In today's wise sayings, two of the big themes of Proverbs emerge again: good vs evil, and attitudes to wealth.

👁 Read Proverbs 11 v 18–23

ENGAGE YOUR BRAIN

▶ What are some of the differences between godly and ungodly people? (v18, 20)

▶ What's the outlook for these two groups of people? (v19, 21)

👁 Read verses 30–31

▶ In what ways are people rewarded in this life? (v31)

▶ What's the result of living a "right" life for God? (v30)

THINK IT OVER

▶ Is your life noticeably different from non-Christians around you?

▶ Do you try to "win souls" and show people what true life is?

PRAY ABOUT IT

Ask God to transform you into someone who clearly serves Him — someone who longs to show people the life offered by Jesus. Pray for friends who don't know Jesus yet.

👁 Read verses 24–29

▶ What's the good news for generous people? (v24–26)

▶ And the bad news for greedy hoarders?

It often seems that greedy people do well and prosper. But ultimately, people who only look out for themselves will be left with nothing. Yet God will reward those who are generous and put others first.

THINK IT OVER

▶ How can you be more generous with your money?

▶ How else can you be generous?

PRAY ABOUT IT

Now talk to God about it.

→ TAKE IT FURTHER

More rich pickings on page 120.

62 | Corrections and connections

What's the most common word in Proverbs? Any ideas? Surprisingly, it's not "wisdom" or "righteous" or "wicked". It's "but". Most proverbs are made up of two bits joined by a "but". The but draws a sharp contrast.

👁 **Read Proverbs 12 v 1**
▶ Do you hate being corrected?
▶ Why should we learn to love discipline?
▶ How does God use correction to help us learn and grow?

👁 **Read verses 2–14** Use these verses to fill in the table below.

GODLY PEOPLE	UNGODLY PEOPLE

THINK IT OVER
▶ What causes goodness or wickedness?
▶ What is God's attitude to them and what are the consequences?
▶ Is there anything you need to talk to God about today?

→ **TAKE IT FURTHER**
No *Take it further* today.

63 | Sharp words

A little boy wanted to know how long the worm in a toothpaste tube was. So he did some research. He got it to stretch right round the bathroom, across the hall and into his parents' room.

Then he decided he'd better put it back in the tube. Oh dear. Bit of a problem...

Read Proverbs 12 v 15–19

▷ *How can our words have long-lasting effects? (v18)*

▷ *What else do we learn about words in these verses?*

Once something's been said (or texted), it's impossible to take it back, just like the boy's toothpaste. And the damage can be long-lasting.

THINK IT OVER

▷ *Think over conversations you've had in the last 24 hours. Did you say anything reckless, untrue, foolish or hurtful?*

▷ *Anyone you need to say sorry to?*

▷ *Think of specific ways this week that you can...
...be more truthful;
...say wise and helpful things;*

*...stop using words that wound;
...use words to heal.*

Read verses 20–21, 23–28

▷ *Any of these proverbs strike a chord with you?*

▷ *Anything you need to do or say?*

GET ON WITH IT

In your own words, write a proverb to summarise what you've learned today. Remember to put a "but" in the middle!

PRAY ABOUT IT

Talk to God about your use of words.

→ TAKE IT FURTHER

A few more words are on page 120.

64 | More wise words

One more shot of Proverbs today before we jump into Mark's Gospel and search for the real Jesus.

👁 Read Proverbs 13 v 1–12

Look at each of today's proverbs, working out what point each one is making. Also think what action we should take in response.

VERSE	POINT	ACTION

THINK IT OVER

▷ *What have you learned today?*
▷ *What do you need to do and what will you pray about?*

→ TAKE IT FURTHER

Hopeful stuff on page 121.

Mark

True identity

Imagine you met a little old lady in her eighties, wearing a hat and some expensive jewellery. What would you do? Probably ignore her. Maybe giggle at her hat. Perhaps even think about stealing some jewels.

Now imagine that you found out that the old lady is Elizabeth II, Queen of the United Kingdom, Canada, Australia and lots of other places. That should change how you treat her! If you're one of her subjects, you'd need to bow or curtsy and call her "Your Majesty".

How we treat someone shows who we think they are. And this section of Mark's Gospel is all building up to one massive question about who someone is: "Who do you say I am?" (Mark 8 v 29)

It was Jesus who was asking, and it was His followers who had to answer. But in a way, everyone all through history has had to answer the question, as they look at Jesus: "Who is he?"

In Mark 5–8, we'll see people answering that question differently. Is Jesus just a carpenter? A miracle-working prophet? A trouble-maker? A fake? A king? Is He… God?

How can we know? Well, Mark's not just going to challenge us to decide who Jesus is, he's going to give us loads of evidence about Jesus' identity. And, at the same time, we'll see how people treating Jesus very differently, from disliking and distrusting Him to loving and serving Him. Because who they think He is is shown in how they treat Him.

So who is Jesus? That's a question we all have to answer, not just with our lips but in our hearts. It's one of life's big questions. In fact, it's eternity's biggest question. In each episode, in a different way, Jesus is going to be asking you:

"Who do you say I am?"

65 | A terrifying man

Is there anything more terrifying than meeting a man in the grip of real evil? Apparently, there is...

👁 Read Mark 5 v 1–13

Jesus has just calmed a storm (4 v 35–41). But if His disciples think the day's terror is over, they're wrong...

▶ *What's wrong with the man they meet on shore? (v2–5)*

▶ *But who actually seems afraid? (v6–10)*

The demons' destructive abilities are shown by what happens to the pigs they're sent into (v13). But Jesus' life-giving power beats them easily. No wonder they are scared!

▶ *Imagine you live nearby, and hear what Jesus has done. How would you react?*

👁 Read verses 14–20

▶ *What's surprising about the reaction of the locals? (v15–17)*

They're more afraid of the presence of the Lord than they are of the presence of evil.

▶ *What's the right way to respond to Jesus? (v18–20)*

GET ON WITH IT

Jesus has authority over everything. But we'd often prefer Him to leave us alone to get on with our comfortable lives, instead of letting Him be our Lord and live His way.

▶ *Are you stopping Jesus being in charge of some area of your life, because it's easier that way?*

▶ *Will you trust Jesus with that area right now, and live His way?*

THE BOTTOM LINE

Jesus has power. Don't be scared of it; welcome it.

→ TAKE IT FURTHER

Don't be terrified; go to page 121.

66 | Help...

...I need somebody, and not just anybody.

👁 **Read Mark 6 v 21–24**

ENGAGE YOUR BRAIN

▶ What is Jairus' job? What is his problem? (v22–23)

He's a respected, religious man. But not proud. And he knows he needs Jesus. So he "fell at his feet" (v22).

PRAY ABOUT IT

We're often much slower to fall at Jesus' feet and ask for His help. We like to think we can cope by ourselves. Are there things you're worrying about that you need to trust Jesus with? Are there things you're relying on yourself to do that you need to ask Jesus for help with?

👁 **Read verses 25–34**

The woman's bleeding (v25) would have left her constantly unclean by Jewish law, an outcast from God's people. And no one can help (v26).

▶ What does the woman do? And why? (v27–28)

▶ What happens? (v29)

Jesus has made her able to live as part of God's people again. But it's not the end of the story. Jesus keeps asking who touched Him (v30–32).

▶ What does Jesus then say to the woman? (v34)

The woman needs to realise it wasn't reaching out her hand that meant she was healed; it was the faith that caused her to reach out her hand. Jesus responds to people's faith by making them part of God's people.

PRAY ABOUT IT

Thank Jesus that He does what no one else can: make people like you part of God's eternal people.

THE BOTTOM LINE

Jesus can help. So ask.

→ **TAKE IT FURTHER**

The Jesus helpline — page 121.

67 | Dead sleepy

Jesus was on the way to see a dying girl when He stopped to speak to a woman. Big mistake...

Read Mark 5 v 35–36

ENGAGE YOUR BRAIN

▷ What has happened while Jesus was talking? (v35)

▷ Why might Jesus' words in v36 have seemed ridiculous to Jairus?

Read verses 37–43

This girl really is dead. So why does Jesus say what He does in v39? Because while to us death is final and irreversible, to Jesus bringing life to the dead is just like waking someone from their sleep.

▷ How much effort does it take Jesus to raise this dead girl? (v41)

▷ What does this tell us about Jesus?

THINK IT THROUGH

In His dealings with the sick woman and the young girl, Jesus is showing us two things:

- He has the power to bring people into God's people, and the power to give life beyond death.

- He sometimes lets people get beyond all hope before He steps in to help, so that they learn not to be afraid, but to believe (v36).

PRAY ABOUT IT

Are there things in your life that you are despairing about? Or terrified about? Are there things you have been struggling with for a long time? Thank Jesus that He cares. Thank Jesus that He has the power to sort those things out. Thank Jesus that He might not sort them out today, so that you can learn to trust Him more.

THE BOTTOM LINE

Jesus has power over death — trust Him!

→ TAKE IT FURTHER

Sleepwalk over to page 121.

68 | Hometown hero?

**Our world is obsessed with appearance.
But appearances can be deceptive.**

👁 Read Mark 6 v 1–2

ENGAGE YOUR BRAIN

▶ *Where is Jesus and what does He do?*

▶ *How do people respond? (v2)*

"Amazed" in the Gospels doesn't mean "wowed" — often, it means "quite confused". So what's wrong with what Jesus is saying? Is He having an off day?

👁 Read verses 2–6

The people realise Jesus is special; He can even do miracles (v2). How wonderful to have Him in their town!

▶ *But what do they also know about Jesus? (v3)*

The problem isn't with Jesus, it's with the people. They think they know who Jesus is — a guy who grew up with them, whose family they know. They can't get their heads round who Jesus really is — a miracle-working messenger from God. Instead of loving and welcoming Him, they're offended by Him.

THINK IT OVER

Many people today make their minds up about Jesus, and then refuse to consider who He says He is.

Are you letting Jesus tell you who He is, what He's like, and what He expects of you — or are you wanting to tell Him?

When you read Jesus' words, do you read them as just a man's ideas, which you're free to reject... or as God's words, whose commands you need to obey?

THE BOTTOM LINE

Let Jesus tell you who He is.

→ TAKE IT FURTHER

Go home via page 121.

69 Working for the king

So far, Jesus has done His kingdom work Himself.
Now, He starts to delegate...

👁 **Read Mark 6 v 7–13**

ENGAGE YOUR BRAIN
▶ *What does Jesus give His 12 disciples the ability to do? (v7)*

This was one of the signs that God's King had come to set up His kingdom; a perfect place where evil is banned.

And the disciples won't need suitcases! Jesus wants them to rely on God, not themselves or their money (v8–9). They're to stay in the first house that welcomes them (v10), rather than move to a nicer one if their teaching is popular. And Jesus warns them that sometimes people won't welcome them or listen to them (v11).

▶ *How do the disciples respond? (v12–13)*

THINK IT OVER
Jesus' people today may not be expected to drive out evil spirits, but we are given the job of telling people about the love and mercy of the Lord Jesus. We're told to encourage people to turn away from sin and turn to Jesus as our King (v12).

Working for Jesus won't make you rich or popular. If you're trying to point people to Jesus with your life and words, don't be surprised if it's tough — it always has been. But what a privilege! Jesus lets us be part of the way He brings people into His kingdom.

GET ON WITH IT
▶ *Are you doing your job?*

▶ *How could you do it more effectively?*

PRAY ABOUT IT
Tell God about three people you want to tell about Jesus. Ask Him to give you the chance, and courage.

➡ **TAKE IT FURTHER**
Get to work... on page 122.

70 ¦ Do the right thing

Sometimes we have to make a choice between being courageous and being cowardly.

👁 Read Mark 6 v 14–20

ENGAGE YOUR BRAIN

John the Baptist was a messenger from God, and the support act to Jesus. John came first, telling people that God's King was on His way.

▶ *What had happened to John since Jesus arrived? (v17)*
▶ *Why? (v17–18)*

So Herodias, who had left her husband Philip to get together with his brother Herod, wants John dead.

▶ *Why doesn't Herod just kill him then? (v20)*

John has done what's right, instead of what's easy. The question is: will Herod do the same?

👁 Read verses 21–29

▶ *How does Herodias get Herod to kill John?*
▶ *Has Herod decided to do what's easy, or to do what's right?*

THINK IT OVER

John's courageous; Herod's a coward. Every day, we have moments where we can do what's easy, or what's right; be like Herod, or like John. And listening to God and doing what's right is hard; it often means losing out. But it's what God's people do.

▶ *Are there any ways you need to stop doing what's easy and start doing what's right?*

Ask God for His help now!

▶ *How does John end up? (v29)*

Remember, he's the one who comes before Jesus. And his death — killed by powerful people who don't like His message — is a little glimmer of what will happen to Jesus.

→ TAKE IT FURTHER

Want more? Try page 122.

71 | Food for thought

**This episode ISN'T about learning to share.
It IS about who Jesus is.**

👁 Read Mark 6 v 30–34

Jesus sees these people as "sheep without a shepherd" (v34). Humans need leading, just like sheep do. Without a leader who knows what we're doing, we'll just be guessing, wandering off, getting hurt. Jesus is the shepherd. He teaches people how to live.

👁 Read verses 35–44

▷ What's the problem? (v35)
▷ What solution does Jesus offer? (v37)

Problem is: they can't (v37)! It's impossible for them to provide for all these people when all they have is five loaves and two fish (v38).

▷ What is Jesus able to do? (v41)
▷ How do the people feel? (v42)

In the Old Testament, when God's people were in the desert, God provided miraculous food for them to eat (Exodus 16 v 1–18). Now, these thousands of people (5000 men,

plus women and children) are in "a remote place" (v35).

▷ And who provides what for them?

THINK IT OVER
▷ What does it teach us about who Jesus is?
▷ What does this episode teach us about what Jesus can do for people?

GET ON WITH IT
▷ What do you look to to tell you how to live?
▷ What do you rely on for what you need in life?
▷ Where do you look for satisfaction?

Make sure it's Jesus, and nothing and no one else!

→ TAKE IT FURTHER
More thoughts to feast on — p122.

85

72 | Lakewalk

Who is Jesus?
And what difference does He make in your life?

👁 Read Mark 6 v 45–56

Remember, several of Jesus' disciples are fishermen. And they're rowing hard, but because of the wind they're getting nowhere (v48).

ENGAGE YOUR BRAIN

▷ *What's amazing about what happens next? (v48–49)*

▷ *Why is the disciples' reaction in v49–50 understandable?*

Jesus' answer in v50 is literally: "Take courage! I AM. Don't be afraid." Flick back to **Exodus 3 v 11–15**, where the God who made everything is speaking to Moses.

▷ *What is the name of the God of creation? (v14)*

And this is what Jesus calls Himself! He's not simply a prophet, or a teacher, or a healer, or a leader. Who is He?

PRAY ABOUT IT

Thank Jesus for who He is. Thank Him that He is the Creator God, who can walk on water.

▷ *What does Jesus do next? (v51)*

▷ *What is the result? (v51, 53)*

THINK IT OVER

Having God in their boat makes all the difference. But notice that Jesus doesn't come and help them immediately (v48). He's teaching them about the Christian life. It involves knowing and trusting and waiting for the all-powerful God.

PRAY ABOUT IT

Tell Jesus about difficulties you're facing. Ask Him to take you through them. Tell Him you trust Him to know when to take them away. Ask Him to help you trust Him as they continue.

→ TAKE IT FURTHER

More reaction on page 122.

73 Acting stupid

Today's section is a lesson in how we can be really religious... and really wrong... and really rejected by Jesus.

👁 Read Mark 7 v 1–5

ENGAGE YOUR BRAIN

▶ *Who is keeping more religious rules — the Pharisees, or Jesus' disciples?*

The Pharisees took obeying God really seriously. They added loads more laws onto the ones God had given.

👁 Read verses 6–13

▶ *What does Jesus call them? (v6)*

This word literally means "actors". Actors pretend to be one person on the outside, when inside they're very different.

▶ *How are the Pharisees acting? (v6)*

And in adding loads of extra laws, they've forgotten about the ones God cares about (v8)! For example, they've set up a system called "Corban", where people save their money for God; but then they let people use it as an excuse for not helping their parents (v10–12).

THINK IT OVER

Pharisees look good. If they were members of your church, they'd be there every week... take notes during sermons... volunteer for jobs. But their "hearts would be far" from Jesus. What counts isn't following traditions or keeping extra laws — it's being a disciple, a follower, of Jesus.

GET ON WITH IT

Have a good look inside. Do you have a heart which loves Jesus, knows Jesus, and wants to follow Jesus?

THE BOTTOM LINE

Be a Jesus-follower, not a Pharisee.

→ TAKE IT FURTHER

Stop acting about; go to page 122.

74 | Inside out or outside in?

The Pharisees' mistake was getting things outside in. Jesus wanted to turn it inside out. Confused? Read on...

👁 Read Mark 7 v 14–15

ENGAGE YOUR BRAIN

▷ *What can't make us "unclean"? (v15)*

▷ *What does make someone unclean? (v15)*

Why does uncleanness matter? Because God is "holy" — totally, whiter-than-white clean. Just as muddy shoes don't belong on a clean carpet, so unclean people don't belong with God or in His perfect eternal heaven.

👁 Read verses 17–23

Jesus repeats His point. It's not things on the outside going into us that matter; it's what's inside us, that comes out of us.

▷ *What kind of things come "inside-out", from our hearts? (v21–22)*

"Malice" means wanting to hurt others; "slander" means saying hurtful things; "folly" means doing things that hurt ourselves.

THINK IT OVER

▷ *Look at v22, and then at your heart. Which of Jesus' words describe you?*

If our problem was outside-in... if the problem was behaviour, or culture, or grubby hands... we could just change how we live, and become clean enough for God. But Jesus says the problem is inside, in our hearts. And you can't change your own heart.

But God can! He can "give you a new heart and put a new spirit in you" (Ezekiel 36 v 26). When someone trusts in His Son, He cleans their heart so they can live with Him. Brilliant!

THE BOTTOM LINE

Our problem is our hearts.
So God gives His people new ones.

➔ TAKE IT FURTHER

Take heart and turn to page 123.

75 | Crumbs of comfort

Today we meet someone who knows they're unclean... who knows they don't deserve God's help... but who doesn't despair.

👁 Read Mark 7 v 24–26

ENGAGE YOUR BRAIN
Jewish Jesus is in non-Jewish, Gentile country. Jesus is not with God's ancient people.

▶ *Why does the woman need Jesus' help? (v25)*

▶ *Where is she from? (v26)*

In other words, non-Jewish, Gentile. Not part of God's ancient people. She's spiritually unclean, she has a daughter who is in the grip of evil... but she begs for Jesus' help.

👁 Read verses 27–30
▶ *Does anything surprise you about how Jesus responds? (v27)*

"Children" = Jews.
"Dogs" = everyone else!

▶ *How does the woman's reply show that she doesn't give up easily? (v28)*

Jesus is testing her humility. Will she accept that she deserves nothing from God? And Jesus is testing her faith. Will she still ask God for what she doesn't deserve? Answer: YES!

THINK IT OVER
▶ *Do you know you're someone with an unclean heart, who deserves nothing from Jesus?*

▶ *Do you know that Jesus is still ready to help you and clean up your life?*

PRAY ABOUT IT
Lord Jesus, I know who I am. I know I have an unclean heart. I don't deserve to be part of Your people, or be helped by You. And I know who You are — God's Son. I know that You have made me part of Your people and helped me, not because I'm good but because You're amazing.

➔ TAKE IT FURTHER
Follow the trail of crumbs to page 123.

89

76 ⋮ How to spot God in a crowd

Hundreds of years before Jesus lived on earth, God had told His people that He would visit them one day. And He'd given them a few ways they could recognise Him...

👁 **Read Isaiah 35 v 3–6**

ENGAGE YOUR BRAIN

▷ *When God comes, what will He do? (v4)*

He's going both to punish sin and rescue His people from that punishment. So it'd be good to know when He's arrived!

▷ *What will happen when God comes to His people? (v5–6)*

In Mark's Gospel, we've already seen the "lame leap like a deer" (Mark 2 v 1–12) — when a man named Jesus healed him. Could Jesus be God? One description down, three to go...

👁 **Read Mark 7 v 31–37**

▷ *By verse 35, how is it "three down, one to go"?*

Verse 37 is more significant than it might seem. Remember, in the Gospels "amazement" normally means "confusion". These people are totally confused! Why? Because Jesus has "done everything well" — He is fitting the description of God-on-earth. Those who are watching might be thinking: "Hey, this guy has done three of the things God will do when He comes. Could He actually be God?"

THINK IT OVER
How does this passage give you great confidence that Jesus really is God? Jesus healed this man with a single word (v34). What does that tell you about Jesus' power?

THE BOTTOM LINE
Jesus did the things God had promised to do.

→ TAKE IT FURTHER
Follow the crowd to page 123.

77 | Cookery class

Yeast is an ingredient in loaves of bread. You put a bit in, and it grows and spreads throughout the bread dough. Jesus says it's dangerous. Huh?!

👁 Read Mark 8 v 1–13

ENGAGE YOUR BRAIN
▶ *What is this episode similar to?*

So, Jesus has just fed 4000 men with a few loaves and fishes. A miracle!

▶ *Why is the Pharisees' request in v11 ridiculous?!*

👁 Read verses 14–21
▶ *What yeast does Jesus warn His disciples to look out for? (v15)*

The Pharisees have seen Jesus' miraculous, God-given signs, but ask for more instead of accepting who He is (v11). Herod listened to John the Baptist's teaching, but decided to ignore it instead of listening to him about Jesus (6 v 20, 27–28). It's easy to be interested in Jesus, without ever acknowledging who He is. Jesus wants His disciples not to fall for this "yeast". This teaching that ignores Jesus and spreads nastily.

▶ *Do the disciples understand what He means? (v16)*

They need to use their eyes and ears (v18). Jesus fed 5000 people with five loaves, and had twelve basketfuls (ie: more than He started with) left (v19)! Then He did it again (v20)! It's obvious who He is!

But they still don't understand (v21).

GET ON WITH IT
It's easy to think: "I'd obey Jesus if there were more evidence" or "I think Jesus' teaching is interesting, but I'm just not sure".

But we have all the evidence we need. Jesus is God. We need to treat Him as our God!

THE BOTTOM LINE
Come up with your own today:

→ TAKE IT FURTHER
More is cooking up on page 123.

78 ┊ The whole picture?

Imagine you see a photo of a woman crying. Sad! But then you look at more than just her face. She's wearing a white dress. She's holding hands with a guy. There are loads of people taking pictures. Happy!

Sometimes, to understand something, you need to see what's around it. Take today's healing, for example.

👁 Read Mark 8 v 22–26

ENGAGE YOUR BRAIN

We've seen Jesus has the power to heal people, calm storms and raise the dead, instantly, with just a word.

- ▶ *What's different about this healing?*
- ▶ *How many times does Jesus put His hands on the man to make a difference?*
- ▶ *What can the man see in his "in-between" stage? (v24)*

At that point, he can see… but also he can't see. Weird!

👁 Read verses 27–29

- ▶ *What questions does Jesus ask? (v27, 29)*

The first question is easy. The second is harder, because the disciples have to make their minds up. It's crunch time. Who is Jesus?

▶ *What does Peter answer? (v29)*

Great! Peter has finally recognised who Jesus is! He can see the truth!

GET ON WITH IT

Who do you say Jesus is — not just with your lips, but in your heart? If you are someone who says Jesus is God's chosen, all-powerful King — the Christ — what difference does it make to your life? Your decisions? Your ambitions?

THE BOTTOM LINE

Jesus is the Christ.

Peter's seen the truth… but we're about to see that he hasn't seen the whole truth. He can see who Jesus is; but he also can't see who Jesus is… More tomorrow.

→ TAKE IT FURTHER

Get a clearer picture on page 123.

79 | Telling Jesus off

Peter knows Jesus is the God's chosen, all-powerful King! But the King says: Don't tell anyone (v30). Why?!

👁 Read Mark 8 v 30–33

ENGAGE YOUR BRAIN
Jesus is the "Son of Man".

▶ *What did Jesus know was going to happen? (v31)*

"Must" is Jesus' way of saying: it's all part of a plan. It's not that He knows these things will unfortunately happen to Him; it's that He's planned for them to happen to Him.

▶ *Jesus is the eternal King, the Christ. Why is v31 shocking?*

▶ *How does Peter react? (v32)*

Peter says: No way! Don't be stupid, Jesus. You're the Christ — you're going to reign in triumph, not die in agony. He tells the Christ off!

In response, the Christ tells Him off (v33). Peter has "in mind … the things of men" — but God's King is different to all other kings. He has come to suffer and die.

THINK IT OVER
Peter thinks he knows better than Jesus what Jesus should do.

▶ *In what ways can you be like Peter?*

▶ *How do you sometimes think Jesus ought to be different, and act differently?*

Peter has seen that Jesus is the King — but not what kind of King He is. He's like the half-blind man from yesterday. That's why Peter mustn't talk about Jesus, because he doesn't yet understand that Jesus is a King who's come to die…

THE BOTTOM LINE
Let Jesus tell you who He is; don't decide who He ought to be!

→ TAKE IT FURTHER
Extra stuff on page 123.

80 | How to follow the king

Take a moment to answer this: **What do you think being a follower of King Jesus involves?**

👁 Read Mark 8 v 34–37

ENGAGE YOUR BRAIN

Jesus is talking to people who are committed to following Him (the disciples); and also to those who are thinking about it (the crowd). Which means that, whoever you are, He's talking to you!

▷ *Jesus is headed for heaven. How can people follow Him there? (v34)*

▷ *What does verse 35 mean, do you think?*

Jesus' point is this: His followers will live completely different lives from everyone else. Instead of doing what's best for them, they'll deny themselves. Instead of holding onto everything they have in life, they'll be happy to lose any of it.

Why? Because followers of Jesus know there's another life to come — and what's the point of having everything for a few decades now, but then losing it all and having nothing for eternity to come (v36)? You might have a life full of achievement and enjoyment, but that won't buy you a place in heaven (v37).

THINK IT OVER

This is hard core. You cannot be a Christian and have a comfortable life. You cannot be a Christian and live like everyone else does.

How did you answer the question at the start? Re-read these verses and answer it based on what Jesus says.

▷ *How do you need to be changed by these verses?*

→ TAKE IT FURTHER

Follow on: page 124.

81 | Ashamed?

I used to be ashamed of my mum's embarrassing footwear. So, if we were together and I saw someone else I knew, I'd walk away from her. I didn't want them to know I was with her. I was ashamed (it's pathetic).

THINK ABOUT IT

▶ Are you ashamed of anyone — something they do, or say (maybe even yourself)?

▶ How does it change the way you treat them?

Read Mark 8 v 38 – 9 v 1

ENGAGE YOUR BRAIN

▶ Who might we be ashamed of? (beginning of v38)

It's hard not to be, because we live in an "adulterous and sinful generation"; a society which loves other stuff more than Jesus, rejects Him, and laughs at His people.

THINK IT OVER

▶ Have you ever been ashamed of Jesus — not stood up for Him in front of others?

▶ Why were you ashamed?

Chances are it was because you didn't want to lose popularity, or comfort — both things that people say we need in life. But remember — Jesus' followers must be willing to lose his [or her] life (v35).

▶ What's the warning in the second half of v38?

That's serious! But let's flip it round: if anyone isn't ashamed of Jesus in front of other people, then when He returns in power to establish His glorious kingdom on earth, He will unashamedly be friends with them.

GET ON WITH IT

How can you stand up for Jesus this week? Pick several specific ways and try to stick to them.

THE BOTTOM LINE

Don't be ashamed of Jesus… and He won't be ashamed of you.

→ TAKE IT FURTHER

Tricky stuff on page 124.

TOOLBOX

Copycat

engage wants to encourage you to dive into God's word, learning how to handle it and understand it more. Each issue, TOOLBOX gives you tips, tools and advice for wrestling with the Bible. This issue, we ask: who should we copy?

FOLLOW THE LEADER?

When learning to drive, it's natural to watch other drivers and copy them. But many experienced drivers don't drive as you're meant to in the driving test. There are some habits you should copy and some you shouldn't.

Sometimes we should follow the example of people in the Bible. But not always! For example...

• In Daniel 6, an order is given that prayers may not be offered to anyone but the king of Babylon. Daniel ignores the king's law and continues to pray to God. Does this mean we should copy Daniel and obey God rather than men?

• In 1 Samuel 3, young Samuel hears his name called during the night. Eli tells Samuel it's God speaking to him which leads to God giving Samuel a prophecy. Does this mean we should expect God to speak to us audibly and tell us what will happen in the future?

• In 2 Samuel 11, King David commits adultery with Bathsheba. This means we too can commit adultery?

What do you think of each of these? I'm guessing you'd probably accept the first one. You might be sceptical about the second one, depending on what you've been taught about how God speaks to us today. Hopefully, we'd all disagree with the third! Yet all three have used the Bible in the same way. We must be careful what we copy. Not everything done by a Bible character is good. And even good things they do may not apply to all Christians at all times.

DESCRIPTION VS PRESCRIPTION

There's a danger in mistaking something the Bible *describes* for something it *prescribes*. The Bible describes what happened to Samuel — God speaking to him in an audible voice. But just because something happened in a particular way to a particular person, it doesn't mean it will happen like that for all of us.

Having said that, we must also be clear that the copycat approach isn't always wrong. Sometimes the Bible does hold up people as examples for us to imitate (or avoid):

"Brothers, as an example of patience in the face of suffering, take the prophets who spoke in the name of the Lord." (James 5 v 10)

"Now these things occurred as examples to keep us from setting our hearts on evil things as they did." (1 Corinthians 10 v 6)

WHO TO COPY?

How can we know whether or not we should copy something in the Bible? Well, we can ask if it fits with or contradicts what is said elsewhere in the Bible. We wouldn't conclude that adultery is acceptable from David's example, because other parts of Scripture clearly teach otherwise.

Another question to ask is: "Does the author intend this description to be copied by the readers?" In Judges 6, God instructs Gideon to fight against His enemies, promising victory. Gideon is doubtful and so asks God to do a couple of specific things to confirm that He wants Gideon to fight (see Judges 6 v 36–40). Some Christians take this as an example for us to follow whenever we need guidance from God, ask Him to make a particular thing happen to indicate what course of action we should take.

The problem with this is that the issue with Gideon wasn't guidance but assurance. He was scared and wanted encouragement from God that He'd give Gideon the victory. So it's unlikely that Gideon's actions are given to us as an example to follow — and the author gives us no indication that they are. What it does show us is that God is very patient with those who have weak faith!

So, when wondering whether or not to copy someone in the Bible, think:
1. Does this action fit with the rest of what the Bible teaches?
2. Does the author intend us to follow this example?

Ideas taken from Dig Deeper by Nigel Beynon and Andrew Sach. Published by IVP and available from The Good Book Company website.

82 Proverbs: Walking God's way

After life-changing from teaching from Jesus, we turn back to Proverbs. But don't get too comfortable because this book is full of life-changing words too. So, if you want to live a life given to God, ask Him to transform you.

👁 Read Proverbs 13 v 13–20

ENGAGE YOUR BRAIN

ᗔ *Why is it good to listen to wise teaching and discipline?*
v13:
v14:
v15:
v18:
v20:

ᗔ *But what if we ignore God's wise words?*
v13:
v15:
v18:
v19:
v20:

Mix with wise people and you'll become wise. Mix with fools (people who reject God) and you'll become not just foolish, but ruined.

👁 Read verses 21–25

I don't think v24 is saying it's OK for parents to batter their children. Punishment and discipline don't have to be physical and certainly shouldn't be violent or motivated by sinful anger. But discipline is important.

When God tells us off — through the Bible or through another Christian — we have to take it on the chin and act on it. Similarly, parents should discipline their children so that they live God's way and don't head down the road to destruction. Real godly discipline is a sign of true love — a desire for the other person to become more like Jesus.

THINK IT OVER

ᗔ *Is God teaching you through any of the other proverbs here?*

PRAY ABOUT IT

Ask God to give you enthusiasm to learn from Him and to hang out with godly, wise people. Pray that you'll accept and learn from His discipline.

→ TAKE IT FURTHER

Search for wisdom on page 124.

83 | Kick off time

Join us for the big match: Wisdom vs Folly. Guess who wins. Before the match, try to define "wisdom" in your own words. And what do you think real folly/foolishness is?

Read verses 1, 3, 6–8, 15–16

ENGAGE YOUR BRAIN

▶ Why do fools lose the match?
v1:
v3:
v6–8:
v15–16:

▶ What does wisdom do for winners?
v3:
v6–8:
v15–16:

True wisdom isn't being clever or successful. Both wisdom and foolishness spring from our attitude to God. We're wise if we have reverence for God and take Him seriously. We're fools if we say He isn't there or ignore Him day by day.

THINK IT OVER

▶ In what ways are you foolish?

▶ How can you be more God-wise in your daily life?

Read v 2, 5, 9, 11, 14, 17

▶ Which of these proverbs hits you hard?

▶ Is there anything that links them together?

▶ If you had to sum them up in one or two proverbs of your own, how would you do it?

PRAY ABOUT IT

▶ Has God been teaching you anything as you read Proverbs?

Try writing a psalm (a song or prayer) to God. Include what He's been teaching you, how you feel about Him and what you're going to do in response. Take your time. And then read it (or sing it!) to God.

→ TAKE IT FURTHER

Missing proverbs found on page 124.

99

84 Cash and character

How would you describe your attitude to money? And what are the main positive and negative characteristics that define you as a person? Hopefully these proverbs will help you answer both of those questions.

👁 Read verses 20–21, 23–24, 31

ENGAGE YOUR BRAIN

▶ Which of these proverbs describes your attitude to money?

▶ How does v20–21 challenge you?

▶ Why does it matter? (v31)

It's easy to tire of people who make demands on our time, energy and money. It can be so much more fun hanging out with people who splash their money around. But we should be generous with our time, money and possessions — being kind to those more "needy" than us. God shows immense love, patience and kindness to needy people like us, so we should do the same (v31).

GET ON WITH IT

▶ How will you put this into practice this week?

👁 Read verses 22, 25, 29–30, 33

In the box below, write down honestly characteristics from these verses that describe you. (Eg. faithful, manipulative, truthful, lying etc.)

PRAY IT THROUGH

Ask God to help you see yourself as you really are. And to be enthusiastic about becoming more like Jesus. Ask Him to shape your attitude to money and to "needy" people you know.

→ TAKE IT FURTHER

Fearful stuff on page 125.

85 ┆ Word of mouth

In this section of Proverbs, there's more on words, discipline, wisdom and loads of other stuff. Before we start, ask God to make it clear what He wants to say to you today.

👁 Read Proverbs 15 v 1–17

GET ON WITH IT

▶ What is God teaching you today?

▶ What do you need to do?

▶ What do you need to stop doing?

▶ How must your attitude change?

▶ What do you need to talk to God about?

ENGAGE YOUR BRAIN

▶ What positive effects can our words have? (v1, 2, 4)

▶ How can words mess things up?

▶ Are you ever guilty of using language like that? (v1, 2, 4)

We must never forget how powerful words are and how deeply they can affect people. Choose your words wisely.

▶ What are we told about people who refuse to be corrected? (v5, 10, 12)

▶ How are you like this sometimes?

▶ Whose correction and discipline should you listen to more?

▶ How can you react better to discipline?

PRAY ABOUT IT

Be totally open and honest with God as you talk about anything He's nudged you about today.

→ TAKE IT FURTHER

More vital stuff on page 125.

86 ¦ Sensible sayings ¦

Time for more proverbs. Which means it's time to ask God to teach, correct and encourage you again. But be warned: if you ask Him, then that's what He'll do!

👁 Read Proverbs 15 v 18–28

ENGAGE YOUR BRAIN

▷ Which proverbs sound most like you?

▷ Which one could you stick on your wall as a motto?

▷ Which one will you share with a friend?

▷ Which one makes no sense?

▷ Who will you ask to explain it to you?

Read verses 29–33

▷ Any good life lessons here?

▷ Why is it good to be cheerful? (v30)

▷ What's the great news for God's people in v29?

Now read these verses again, out loud, turning each one into a prayer. Thank God that He hears your prayers. Ask Him for good news, discipline, fear and humility.

Here's our quote of the day:
"If you realise that you aren't as wise today as you thought you were yesterday, you're wiser today."

PRAY ABOUT IT

Is Proverbs helping you become more God-wise? Ask God to help you change in one specific way today.

→ TAKE IT FURTHER

No *Take it further* today.

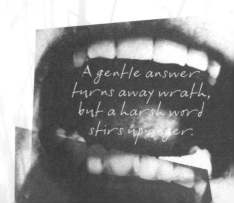

A gentle answer turns away wrath, but a harsh word stirs up anger.

87 | The Master's masterplan

When you're worried, when things don't seem to be working out, when friends or family don't care much, when it feels the world's going mad around you... what big truth can reassure Christians?

Read Proverbs 16 v 1–9

ENGAGE YOUR BRAIN

▶ *What's the truth we can cling on to in hard times? (v3–4, 9)*

Invigorating, huh? God has the last word. Ultimate control is in His hands. There's a limit to human wisdom: so even the wisest people must recognise that God's in charge. We make plans, do our work, decide a hundred things each day, or just go with the flow. But, whatever we do, God's in control. He's sovereign.

That's hugely reassuring — and it's true no matter how things appear. The Bible says we're to believe both that God's in control and that we're free to make choices. Hard to grasp? Well, we make plans and God over-rules (v1). We take action, but must commit everything to God (v3). We think we know where we're going, but God directs our path (v9).

THINK IT OVER

▶ *Does life just seem to be chance?*

▶ *Are there situations where God seems not to be in control?*

▶ *What decisions do you have to make soon that scare you?*

Read verses 1, 3 and 9 again. Take heart that God knows, cares, rules.

PRAY ABOUT IT

Pray about what's on your mind. Talk to God about any worries or plans/decisions you're making. Ask Him for guidance and thank Him that He's in control and will do what's best for you.

THE BOTTOM LINE

The Lord is in total control.

→ TAKE IT FURTHER

The king's speech — page 125.

88 | Final words of wisdom

It's the final visit to Proverbs this issue. Have you been allowing God to teach you and change you? Or have you been resisting His life-changing wisdom? If you mean it, ask Him to speak powerfully to you today.

👁 Read Proverbs 16 v 16, 19

▶ How important is it to have loads of money?

▶ What's it better to have? (v16)

▶ How has Proverbs changed your attitude to wealth?

👁 Read verses 23–24, 27–28

▶ What are we told about using language positively? (v23–24)

▶ Have you been like v27 or v28 recently?

▶ So what do you need to do?

👁 Read verses 17, 20, 32

▶ What other tips for godly living are we given?

▶ Which one do you need to act on?

👁 Read verses 18, 21–22, 29–31

▶ Which of these proverbs don't you understand?

▶ Look at it more carefully — what do you think it means?

▶ How could you find out?

GET ON WITH IT

▶ What's the main thing God has been teaching you from Proverbs?

▶ What action do you need to take?

▶ How exactly will you do that?

PRAY ABOUT IT

Spend extra time talking to God about what He's put on your heart and mind.

→ TAKE IT FURTHER

A few more wise words on page 125.

The fear of the Lord teaches a man wisdom, and humility comes before honour.

89 | Hairy stuff

We complete this issue of Engage with two short and sweet psalms. Today we focus on Aaron's beard. Yes, really.

👁 **Read Psalm 133**

▷ *What does David think is totally brilliant? (v1)*

▷ *What does he say it's as good as? (v2)*

▷ *What else? (v3)*

▷ *What is promised to God's united people? (v3)*

God chose Aaron to be His priest. It was such an important role it was marked by Moses pouring precious oil over Aaron's head until it ran down his beard and onto his special robes (Leviticus 8 v 5–12). It was a sign of him being set aside to serve God. It was a great moment.

David says it's great when believers are united, serving God. Christians are set aside as God's chosen people — one sign of this is God's diverse people working together in unity. Like the flowing oil, God's blessings flow to His united people.

Mount Hermon was well known for having lots of dew, which helped plants to grow. If such dew fell on Mount Zion (Jerusalem, a symbol of God's people), it would be really fruitful. When believers are united and work together, they'll be fruitful together and will be blessed by God. They will receive the greatest blessing of all — eternal life with God (v3).

GET ON WITH IT

▷ *Which believers do you not "live together in unity" with?*

▷ *How can you become closer and more united?*

▷ *How can you serve God together (even if you don't like each other)?*

PRAY ABOUT IT

Think about what verse 1 means for you and your life and pray about it.

→ **TAKE IT FURTHER**

Oil for one and one for oil: page 125.

90 | Encouraging words

This is the last of the songs of ascents, which God's people sang on their way up to Jerusalem. Actually, this one is a sung conversation between the worshippers at God's temple and the Levites (temple servants).

👁 Read Psalm 134

ENGAGE YOUR BRAIN

▶ *What do the people tell the Levites to do? (v1)*

▶ *When?*

▶ *How and where? (v2)*

▶ *How do the Levites reply? (v3)*

The people who've been worshipping are on their way home, but some of the priests and Levites will be staying in the temple all night, continuing the worship. So the people are encouraging them to keep going and to keep praising God.

The temple workers respond by saying: May the Creator of the universe bless you! Nice. What a good blessing. It may seem weird to sing to each other but it must have been encouraging for both sides of the "conversation".

"Keep praising God and working for Him — you're doing a great job!"
"Thanks, may God bless you loads!"
Smiles all round.

GET ON WITH IT

▶ *Think of 3 Christian workers and how you'll encourage them:*
   1.

   2.

   3.

SHARE IT

Convert this psalm into modern language that relates to your life and the Christians you know. If you like the result, send it to someone to encourage them.

PRAY ABOUT IT

Now spend time praising God!

→ TAKE IT FURTHER

No *Take it further*. So use the time to order the next issue of *engage!*

TAKE IT FURTHER

If you want a little more at the end of each day's study, this is where you come. The TAKE IT FURTHER sections give you something extra. They look at some of the issues covered in the day's study, pose deeper questions, and point you to the big picture of the whole Bible.

DANIEL
Dare to be different

1 – CONTROLLING INTEREST
Read 1 Thessalonians 5 v 23–24

▶ What does Paul pray for the Thessalonians?

▶ How can he be sure God will answer his prayer?

▶ How does it encourage you to know that God can and will keep you following Him?

Read Philippians 1 v 4–6
and thank God for that promise.

2 – FOOD FOR THOUGHT
So where should we draw the line? Some Christians make a stand by choosing not to watch "18" or "R" rated movies (even if they're old enough). Some decide not to drink alcohol. Some always make sure they have a Christian friend with them when they go to a party, to keep an eye on them. These aren't rules for all of us — but it's where some believers have chosen to draw the line.

▶ Do people know you're a Christian?

▶ How?

▶ Do you need to make more of a stand in certain situations?

▶ Be specific. Write down something you'll change...
a) at home.
b) among Christian friends.
c) among non-Christian friends.

3 – NIGHTMARE SITUATION
▶ How would you use this passage to answer a friend who believes in dream interpretation/horoscopes/tarot readings etc?

▶ Why is God the only one who knows the past, present and future?

4 – THE INTERPRETER
Read Romans 13 v 1–7

▶ Who is ultimately behind all governments and authorities? (v1, 2, 4, 6)

▶ How are authorities supposed to behave? (v3–4)

▶ What authorities are there in your life? Teachers? Parents? Police? Government? Boss?

ⓘ *What is your attitude towards them?*
ⓘ *Do these verses change anything?*

Read 1 Peter 2 v 16–17

ⓘ *Can you spot any differences between how we are to treat the "king"/government and God?*
ⓘ *What will that mean when governments want us to go against God's laws?*

5 – FEEL THE HEAT

Maybe Shadrach and the guys knew this promise from the prophet Isaiah; he would have written it around the same time they were taken into exile.

Read Isaiah 43 v 1–4

This is how God treats His people despite the way they've treated Him. Incredible. Read through these verses again, carefully. Think about how these words are true for Christians today. Then tell God how you feel about that.

6 – GOD RULES

Read **Acts 9 v 1–31** and **1 Timothy 1 v 12–17** for another example of how God can call anyone at all into His family.

7 – GOD'S GRAFFITI

Read 2 Peter 3 v 3–10

God always gives people a chance to repent; even people as proud and foolish as Belshazzar. Spend some time praying for people you know who haven't yet turned back to God as their King.

8 – LION AND CHEATING

Use **verses 26–27** to answer the following:

ⓘ *Does God exist?*
ⓘ *Is He in control?*
ⓘ *How long for?*
ⓘ *Does He do anything in the world?*
ⓘ *Does He have the ability to change things?*
ⓘ *Does He care about people?*

Think how Jesus' coming to earth answers those questions even more clearly. And it's Jesus who performed God's great rescue — saving us from sin and hell and securing forgiveness and eternal life.

1 JOHN

Real Christianity

9 – GET THE MESSAGE

Read Genesis 1 v 1, then John 1 v 1, and 1 John v 1

ⓘ *What do they have in common?*
ⓘ *So what's at the heart of the message of the whole Bible?*

Now read 1 John 1 v 3–4, then 2 John v 4, and 3 John v 4

ⓘ *What brings John joy?*
ⓘ *So what should make us happy?*
ⓘ *How should this affect what we do and say?*

10 – TRAVELLING LIGHT

Light is a strange thing. Put a bright light outside at night and moths and other bugs will come and gather round it. For other animals, light is danger; they'll stay away from the light and stick to the safety of the shadows. As with light, so it is with Jesus — the light of the world.

Read 1 John 1 v 5–7 and then John 3 v 19–21

We are not naturally like the moths. We do not like the light. Instead we prefer to walk in the darkness and ignore God. Sometimes we may claim to love God, but are really walking in darkness. Use **1 John 1 v 6** now to check your own "walk" and pray to God about it.

11 – SIN SOLUTION

Not sure what Jesus commands us? Check these out:
Matthew 5 v 42, 44; 6 v 3–4, 9, 26; 7 v 12.

🔁 *Which of these do you need to work on?*

🔁 *What exactly will you do about it?*

Ask God's help, through the Holy Spirit.

12 – OH BROTHER!

In his letter, John tells us what marks out a true Christian. Those who are truly in touch with God...
a) recognise and confess their sin.
   (1 John 1 v 6–10)

b) seek to love and obey Jesus.
   (1 John 2 v 1–6)
c) show genuine love to other Christians
   (1 John 2 v 7–14).
🔁 *How are you doing with a, b and c?*

14 – WORLDS APART
Read James 4 v 4–6
🔁 *What's the truth for anyone who goes the world's way and lives to please themselves? (v4)*
🔁 *What must we remember about God? (v6)*

"Adulterous people" is a common Bible term for people who've betrayed their promises and turned from God. We can't be a friend of God and a friend of the world — behaving the same way a society that rejects God behaves. Yet we keep living as if we can. We may have an inbuilt capacity for wrong (v5), but God gives all the help we need to resist it (v6). The only treatment is total repentance.

15 – ANTICHRISTS
Read verse 22 again
If Jesus wasn't God, then He was only another human being. That means He would have been sinful and His own sin would have needed to be dealt with — He wouldn't be able to pay for anyone else's. For us to be forgiven, it needed the sinless Son of God to deal with our sin. And He did. On the cross.

16 – FAMILY LIKENESS

Read 1 John 2 v 28

Will you meet Jesus with regret, embarrassment, fear, anticipation, confidence, or what? Someone wise said: "Our present attitude to His coming gives some idea of whether or not we're ready to meet Him."

Read 1 John 3 v 1

John wants us to see that God's love is in a completely different category to any human love. If we fail to accept God's love for us personally, then we're left always trying to be good enough to persuade God to love us. And that's impossible.

▷ *What will it mean to be a child of God — now and in the future?*

17 – SIN BIN

Read verse 6

Christians show they're truly grateful for Jesus' death (which took away sin, v5) by not keeping on sinning. Born of God (v9), it's now become unnatural to continue sinning. Top quote: "We can't expect to be confident on the day we see Christ if we're complacent about sin in our lives now."

▷ *Point made? How does it hit you?*

18 – KIDS' TALK

Read Matthew 6 v 25–34

▷ *What's the problem with worrying? (v27)*

▷ *How does Jesus reassure His followers? (v26–32)*

▷ *What should our priority be? (v33)*

▷ *How do you fail to trust God?*

▷ *Do you hedge your bets by trusting in good exam results, getting a good job etc?*

Jesus says there are only two sorts of ambition. Either you can be self-centred or God-centred. Tell God what yours is. Ask for God's help to trust Him and not to worry.

DANIEL

20 – BEAST BEHAVIOUR

Daniel chapters 7–12 is a bit like Revelation. Full of surprising pictures, big numbers, strange symbols and some intriguing details. It reveals the greatness of God in a memorable way.

One hint: don't get stuck trying to figure out what all the symbols represent. Even Daniel didn't get to the bottom of it. See 10 v 12. What did Daniel do as he tried to understand what he saw? He used his mind — and he prayed to God. That's a good principle for us, wanting to understand God's word.

Read 2 Timothy 2 v 7

▷ *How hard do you work at understanding the Bible?*

▷ *What attitude to God do we need to have first?*

21 – THRONE ZONE

"Son of man" is the third most-used title for Jesus in the New Testament (the first is "Christ", the second is "Lord"). But it was Jesus' favourite name for Himself (Mark 2 v 28). It shows that Jesus knew exactly who He was — God in human form.

22 – VICTORY INSIGHT

The book of 1 Peter has loads to say about suffering as a Christian. Start with **1 Peter 4 v 12–16**.

▷ *How should we respond to suffering?*
▷ *Why?*
▷ *What should be the reason for our suffering?*

Now skim through the rest of 1 Peter and see what else you can find about dealing with suffering.

23 – VICIOUS ATTACK

Read verse 14 again
The number 2300 shouldn't necessarily be taken literally. Here's a guideline on the way numbers work in the Bible: if a number has significance that God wants us to know, He'll tell us clearly in the passage. Otherwise, we don't need to worry about it too much. So the point of v14 is this: rebellion towards God may go on for a long time — but it won't go on for ever.

To resist the devil, think about these questions:
▷ *Do I read the Bible regularly?*
▷ *Do I pray?*
▷ *Am I meeting with other Christians?*

If you are, your enemy doesn't stand much of a chance. If you're not, he could just get a foothold.

Read 1 Peter 5 v 8–9
and take these verses to heart.

24 – VISION EXPLAINED

Rebellion towards God knows no limit. It will stop at nothing. Daniel saw what people are capable of. That's why rebellion against God (sin) must be brought to an end. Imagine a world where sin is allowed to run its course: a frightening chaos of unleashed anarchy. God has to act. And He does (v25). God must punish those who rebel against Him. It can't be brushed under the carpet.

▷ *How seriously do you take sin?*
▷ *Does it bother you as much as it bothered Daniel?*

Remind yourself of **Romans 8 v 38–39**. Have you ever memorised it? It's a great thing to remember when times are tough.

25 – PRAY AS YOU LEARN

Read Hebrews 4 v 14–16
▷ *Who brings us close to God?*
▷ *What is He like?*
▷ *On what basis can we approach God in prayer?*
▷ *What are we promised? (v16)*

26 – NUMBER CRUNCHER
Read verses 25–27 again

God would keep His promise to rebuild Jerusalem. He would forgive His people for turning away from Him and they would live His way again (v25). After Jerusalem was rebuilt, God's chosen King, ("Anointed One") would come. That's Jesus. But He would be violently killed (v26). Then Jerusalem and God's temple would be destroyed again. Sacrifices to God would end (v27), because Jesus was the ultimate sacrifice. He died so that people can have their sins forgiven. They can now go straight to God for forgiveness. They don't need to offer sacrifices anymore!

I'm not sure exactly what the "abomination that causes desolation" / "Awful Horror" / "destroyer" in v27 is. But other Bible bits show that it's set up by God's enemy to turn God's people away from Him. But God has already ordered its end.

There's loads of tricky stuff in these verses, but remember the most important thing — JESUS is at the centre of God's plans. His death makes it possible for anyone to turn back to God and have their sins forgiven. Thank God for sending Jesus to rescue His people so they can be with God again.

27 – SHINING EXAMPLE
Check out verses 13–14 again

It's not just humans who have wars. There's a spiritual war going on too. The devil and his demons (and people who reject God) fight God, His people and His angels. Jesus was busy with all this, but He hadn't forgotten Daniel's prayer!

28 – WAR STORIES
Read Ephesians 6 v 10–18

God told Daniel to be strong. This part of Ephesians tells us how to be strong. And why we need to be.

▶ *Who is our enemy and how does he work? (v11–12)*

▶ *How strong is our opposition?*

Verses 13–18 list the spiritual protection God provides for His people.

▶ *Are you wearing it?*

▶ *If so, which bits need servicing?*

29 – RISE AND FALL
Read Philippians 2 v 5–11

▶ *What was the end result for this evil king who exalted himself? (Daniel 11 v 45)*

▶ *What was the end result for Jesus, our King who humbled Himself?*

▶ *Where is Jesus right now and what's His status? (v9)*

▶ *What will happen one day? (v10–11)*

This is the Jesus who died on the cross for people — the same Jesus who is now more powerful than we can imagine. He is God's all-powerful King! One day everyone will recognise who He is (v10–11), whether the spiritual world (*in heaven*), His saved people (*on earth*), or those who opposed and rejected Him until it was too late (*under the earth*).

30 – THE END?

There are a lot of echoes of Daniel in the book of Revelation. See how many you can spot — check out **Revelation 20 v 11 – 21 v 4**.

31 – WISE AND FALL

Read Revelation 22 v 11–13

▷ *Spot any similarities with today's Daniel chapter?*

We still don't know exactly when the world will end, although we know now that it will happen when Jesus returns. Until then we can be confident that God is utterly in control. While we wait there will be many who turn to Jesus in faith and are purified, made spotless and refined (Daniel 12 v 10) but others who will sadly continue to rebel against God until the end.

1 JOHN

32 – REAL CHRISTIANITY

Read John 15 v 18 – 16 v 4

▷ *What did Jesus say His followers should expect? (v18–20)*
▷ *Why shouldn't this surprise them? (v18)*

Christians are different. We're to live in a way that honours God, not just be the same as everyone else. The world will hate us for this, just as they hated Jesus.

▷ *Who helps believers tell people about Jesus? (v26–27)*
▷ *Why did Jesus warn His disciples they'd be persecuted? (16 v 1)*

Jesus told them straight — you're going to suffer for following me. He warned them because He wanted them to keep trusting Him through hard times and not abandon Him when the heat got turned up (v1). He knew all about it and was in control. And Jesus gave His Spirit to help us spread the gospel (v26).

33 – TRUE LOVE

Read verse 16 again and then Romans 5 v 6–11

▷ *How does God show His love for us? (v8)*
▷ *How would you describe God's timing? (v6)*
▷ *What's true for those who trust in Jesus? (v9)*
▷ *Why can we be sure of this? (v10)*

You may have read stories of people giving their own lives to save loved ones. But God's love shown on the cross beats all human love hands down. We were God's enemies, sinning against Him when He gave His Son to die in our place. If God's done the difficult thing (v10a), of course we can be sure He'll complete the job and hold on to us when His judgment comes (v10b). And there's even more to get excited about (v11).

34 – CONFIDENT CHRISTIANITY

Read 1 John 3 v 13–24

and think, how does...

v13 warn me?

v15 rebuke me?

v16 motivate me?

v17 prepare me?

v18 challenge me?

v19–20 reassure me?

v23 remind me?

v24 encourage me?

35 – THAT'S THE SPIRIT!

Read Matthew 7 v 15–20

▶ *According to these verses, how can we tell if someone is a true follower of Jesus?*

▶ *What is Jesus talking about when He mentions fruit?*

▶ *Why are our actions such a good indication of our hearts?*

The sort of people Jesus is talking about here — false prophets — are the type of people who have power and influence in the church. Imagine you hear a church leader or youth leader completely denying something in the Bible, or see them stealing money, or find out they're always nasty and sarcastic behind people's backs. Their fruit — their actions — shows the reality of their hearts. Now that's not to say our leaders are always going to be perfect, but if the fruit is overwhelmingly bad, so is the tree.

▶ *What is the final outcome for these false prophets? (v19)*

37 – AM I REALLY A CHRISTIAN?

Read verses 13–16 again

This is so vital and so helpful for doubting Christians like us that we're going to look at it again. God gives His Holy Spirit to all Christians, living in them, helping them to serve God (v13). When Christians show unselfish love for others, that's the Holy Spirit at work!

John and the disciples spent time with Jesus (v14).

Do you believe what they say in the Bible about Him?

▶ *And do you tell other people about Jesus?*

▶ *Do you believe that Jesus is God's Son? (v15)*

▶ *Do you believe that He became a human and did incredible miracles?*

▶ *Do you believe that He died and was raised back to life?*

▶ *Have you seen God's love in your life? (v16)*

▶ *Do you know He cares for you?*

▶ *Have you seen Him answer prayers?*

So Christians...

• have God's Spirit helping them to serve God and love others.

• believe what John and the other disciples say about Jesus.

• tell others about Jesus.

• believe that Jesus is God's Son.

• know that God loves them.

38 – FAITH LIFT

Read 1 John 1 v 1–5 again

Evidence of faith in your life: it can't help but lead to... **love** for God and His people (v1); **obedience** to God's commands (v3); and **victory** as we claim Christ's resources to help us live for Him (v5).

▶ *Do you believe Jesus is God's Son?*
▶ *Do you love God?*
▶ *Are you seeking to obey Him?*

If so, that's great 1 John evidence to encourage you that you're born of God and share in His eternal life! Amazing.

39 – SON RISE

Read verses 6–8 again

Water symbolises Jesus' baptism, and blood symbolises His death. Jesus' ministry began with His baptism and led up to His death on the cross. When John was writing this letter, false teachers claimed Jesus was born as human and remained only human (and not God) until His baptism. They claimed that the Christ, the Son of God, descended on the human Jesus at His baptism, but left Him before His suffering on the cross — so it was only the man Jesus who died, not God's Son. Nonsense!

Throughout his letter, John has repeatedly shown that Jesus Christ is God as well as man (1 v 1–4, 4 v 2). John is now telling His readers that Jesus was the Son of God not only at His baptism but also at His death. This is extremely important, because if Jesus died only as a man, His

sacrifice wouldn't have been enough to take away the guilt of human sin.

40 – LIFE ASSURANCE

Re-read verses 14–15 and then read Matthew 7 v 7–12

▶ *What should our attitude be when approaching God? (v7–11)*
▶ *Why is v8 so reassuring?*
▶ *But what do we have to do?*
▶ *What does Jesus remind us about God's character in v11?*

Whether it's a request, a worry or long-term searching, such prayers are answered by God. That's the promise. But they'll be answered in God's way and God's time, and sometimes that means a loud "No" or "Not yet". Think how rubbish it would be if God answered all our prayers the way you wanted. It would make us so selfish.

Do you find it difficult to pray? Do you think that God is too busy, too disappointed by you sinning yet again, or that your needs are so insignificant that He won't listen to you? Read verses 7–11 again and trust your loving, heavenly Father with your needs and worries, as you talk to Him.

41 – WE KNOW, WE KNOW, WE KNOW

Why not take time to read through the whole of 1 John, remembering it's one long letter. Even better if you could read it out loud with another Christian and then chat about it. Grab a notebook and scribble down anything that jumps out at you or puzzles you. Note things that you need to change and stuff you know you should do. And write down things and people you need to pray about.

**Read verse 3 again
and then Isaiah 50 v 6**

▶ *Who is the Isaiah verse about?*

Now read Isaiah 50 v 1–11

God's people thought He had left them, like a husband divorcing his wife. God hadn't abandoned them — they had sinned against God so He rightly punished them, sending them into exile in Babylon. But, incredibly, He would bring them back. Nothing is impossible for God (v2–3).

▶ *God's Servant speaks in v4–10. How is He different from the Israelites? (v4–5)*
▶ *How far was He prepared to go to obey God? (v6)*
▶ *What helped Him cope with such violent opposition? (v7–9)*

The way to make sure you treat God properly is to obey His Servant Jesus' word (v10); to do what He does, whatever you face in life (v4–9). God is more than strong enough to get us through. Relying on yourself (making your own "light", v11) brings God's punishment.

Read verse 8 again

Has this happened yet? Well, yes and no. Jesus has come to redeem sinful people —

to buy them back from slavery to sin and the punishment they deserve. That's why He died on the cross and was raised back to life. And yet it's still to come — one day Jesus will return to gather His people and we'll finally be free from all sin and misery.

EZRA
Going home

**Read verse 1 again
followed by Jeremiah 25 v 11–12
and 29 v 10–14**

It's easy to think of Jeremiah as a prophet of gloom, but he was a messenger of true hope. He urged God's people to pin their hopes on God's great plans for them. Plans for prosperity, forgiveness and a return home. Despite their rebellion, God would listen to His people and give them great things.

Do you ever worry about an uncertain future? For Christians, the future is not uncertain. God promises to forgive His people, to take them home to live with Him and give them more than they could ever deserve. Jeremiah 29 v 11 is a verse worth memorising.

**Read verses 2–4 again
then Leviticus 1 v 1–9**

The burnt offering was the central sacrifice in Old Testament times. It involved:

a) recognising and confessing sin

b) transfer of sin to a substitute, an animal

c) entire destruction of the animal, to show the punishment deserved for the sin, and to symbolise that the anger of God against sin "burnt itself out" on the substitute.

Powerful stuff. One life spared by the death of another. From the offerer's point of view, the sacrifice was costly and had to be made repeatedly. This is what these guys in Ezra 3 v 1–6 were doing — daily coming back to God's mercy.

Jesus offered a once-and-for-all sacrifice for our sin. We're to turn to Him daily, but not with a sacrifice for sin (He's already done that), but with a sacrifice of praise (Hebrews 13 v 15–16).

▷ *Ready to give your all, daily, to praise Jesus?*

▷ *What sins does this mean you must leave behind?*

47 – APPLY SOME FOUNDATION

God's people would now be a distinct community within a world empire. Their distinguishing marks would be:
a) the altar
b) the temple
c) the book (wait for chapter 7...)

Christians today are to live in such a way that we're distinguished from the world by being devoted to God. So we're to worship Him (in the way we live as much as when we meet together), obey His word and be witnesses for Him to others.

▷ *How are you getting on in these three areas?*

48 – THE PLOT THICKENS

Read 2 Timothy 3 v 12

Why are we often surprised or rocked when we get opposed for being Christian? The Bible promises persecution will come. Be a realist. God is for us so who can stand against us? (Romans 8 v 31) But, as with Jesus, through suffering God brings His people to glory.

49 – WORK IN PROGRESS

Haggai 1 v 1–15

▷ *What is the people's excuse for not getting on with the job? (v2)*

▷ *What has their recent experience been like? (v9–11)*

▷ *What reason does God give for all these frustrations? (v9)*

▷ *What's the people's reaction to God's message? (v12)*

▷ *Do you treat God's message in the Bible that way?*

Fearing the Lord doesn't mean becoming a trembling wreck — it means taking Him seriously, recognising that He's in charge.

▷ *What got the people working hard on the temple? (v14)*

▷ *What does that tell us about the source of any of our good deeds?*

50 – CELEBRATION NATION

After the 16-year gap, it took them another three and a half years to complete the temple. Ezra doesn't mention anything that happened during this time. But Haggai does.

Read Haggai 2 v 1–9

▶ *How were the older generation feeling? (v3)*

▶ *How did God encourage the people? (v4–5)*

Do you ever feel that being a Christian now isn't very impressive. Especially not compared to years ago, when there were masses of people turning to Christ, or believers standing up for Jesus even if it meant a gruesome death? But God's promises aren't all in the past (like the one He made when He brought His people out of Egypt, v5). He has promises for them now too.

▶ *What will God do? (v7)*

▶ *Who does everything belong to? (v8)*

The *desired* or *treasure* of all nations in v7 is absolutely true — this temple was built using the king of Persia's funds! It also refers to God's kingdom in the future (Hebrews 12 v 26–29) — when God's people from every nation will become a great kingdom serving the Lord in glory!

51 – EZRA'S ENTRANCE

It's 458BC, during Artaxerxes' reign. By the way, the action in the book of Esther took place in the reign of Xerxes, the king before Artaxerxes and after Darius. Malachi the prophet preached to God's people about 460BC — just before Ezra arrived. Check out Malachi's astounding book, which looks forward to Jesus.

52 – EZRA'S EXODUS

Read Ezra 8 v 24–36

Catch up on the bit we missed out.

53 – WEDDING YELLS

In Ezra's time, the issue was foreigners. For us, it's non–Christians. So what does the New Testament say about marrying non-Christians?

1. For a Christian already married to a non-believer, don't go for divorce. Live a lifestyle that might win them for Christ (1 Corinthians 7 v 12–13 and 1 Peter 3 v 1–7).
2. Marrying a non-believer will endanger your faith and weaken your marriage (2 Corinthians 6 v 14–16).
3. We have a mission to the world which requires Christians to be distinctive (Matthew 5 v 13–16).

What about going out with / dating non-Christians? Principles 2 and 3 (above) apply. The big question Ezra 9 forces us to ask is: "What god does the other person serve?"

▶ *Need to talk over any of these issues with an older Christian?*

55 – SOUL SONG

Make a list of questions you'd like to ask God. As you grow as a Christian, you'll discover answers to some of these.

▶ *Are you prepared to leave the rest in God's hands, trusting Him?*

Read Romans 11 v 33–36

Universities are full of theologians who merely have an academic interest in God. Churches can be full of worshippers who don't often think much.

▶ *What's the warning here?*

▶ *Do you find the right balance between thinking about God and praising Him?*

56 – BACK TO THE FUTURE

Psalm 132 v 11–18 is a poetic version of God's promise in 1 Kings chapter 9.

Read 1 Kings 9 v 1–9

▶ *How did God respond to Solomon's prayer? (v3)*

▶ *What did He tell Sol to do? (v4)*

▶ *What would be the result? (v5)*

▶ *But what was the warning? (v9)*

We shouldn't take God's warnings negatively. God shows great love and kindness in reminding us what we need to do to please Him and the consequences if we don't. Everything was going well for God's king and God's people. But it's often when life's going well that the devil atttacks and we mess up big time. Solomon needed to listen to God's warning in v4–9. And so do we. Sometimes we can cruise through life enjoying it so much that we fail to notice we're no longer obeying God so much. Or He's slipped way down our priorities.

PROVERBS

57 – WALKING GOD'S WAY

We recommend that you read Proverbs chapters 1–9 (we covered them in issue 17). According to chapters 1–9, true wisdom is living life in the God lane. Living the way God wants us to live. Taking God seriously. Chapters 10–31 spell that out in everyday detail. Our hope is that these next chapters will hit you between the eyes, jab you in the ribs and kick you up the backside. That's what Proverbs did for us. And we hope these proverbs will help you get God-wise too.

58 – SHUT YOUR MOUTH!

Read verse 16
and then Romans 6 v 22–23

True freedom isn't doing as we please: it's doing as God pleases. As our master, sin pays us wages (what we deserve) — death. But God as our master gives us a gift (what we don't deserve) — eternal life. Christians now serve a new boss, so they should live in a way that honours God, and not turn back to their old boss, sin.

59 – GOOD VS EVIL

Read verse 25 again
and then Luke 6 v 46–49

▶ *What mistake were some of Jesus' "followers" making? (v46)*

▶ *What's true for people who put His words into practice? (v48)*

▶ *And those who don't? (v49)*

Some people called Jesus "Lord" and yet refused to obey Him and do what He said. Right now there are people who call themselves Christians and yet live only for themselves and ignore Jesus' commands. When Jesus returns as Judge, such people will be washed away. Only those whose lives are built on firm foundations — obeying Jesus — will stand firm through the Day of Judgment.

60 –RICH OR RIGHTEOUS?

Read Ephesians 2 v 6–10

▶ *How are Christians rich? (v7–9)*
Our new life, freedom and rescue are all down to God. We're full of sin, so we don't deserve God's love and rescue. Yet He gives it to us anyway. That's what **grace** is — God sending His Son to die for us despite us deserving His punishment. When we turn to Jesus, God makes us into something new, so that we can serve Him in great ways. And one day we'll live with Him in perfection for ever. That's what it means to be truly rich.

61 – RICH PICKINGS

**Read verses 24–26 again
and then 2 Corinthians 9 v 6–11**

▶ *How should we approach giving our time, talents and money? (v7)*
▶ *Are you a cheerful giver?*
▶ *Who is the most generous giver of all? Hint: look back at 8 v 9!*
▶ *How does God act towards us? (v8–11)*
▶ *When we give away, in what way do we gain more than we give? (v10)*

▶ *What is the end result of giving generously? Is it so people think we're great? (v11)*

Our giving, like our whole lives, should result in praise and thanksgiving towards God. Our purpose is to bring God glory. Thank God for all He has given you and all He continues to give you. Ask Him to help you remember that and to respond with thanksgiving towards Him and with generosity to others.

63 – SHARP WORDS

**Look at verses 19–22
followed by Psalm 52**

▶ *How is David's enemy described?*
▶ *How does God view him? (v1)*
▶ *What will God do with this man? (v5)*
▶ *How would others view him? (v6–7)*

Bullies often seem to prosper. For a while. People who live for themselves and take advantage of others won't succeed in the end. God will destroy them and everyone will see that their sin and riches came to nothing.

▶ *Why can God's people trust Him? (v8)*
▶ *Why should they praise Him? (v9)*
▶ *Where should they put their hope? (v9)*

God's people will live and flourish with God for ever. We may be bullied and downtrodden for a while, but one day that will all change. God's love never fails. We know this because of all He's done for us. Our hope in Him is certain.

64 – MORE WISE WORDS
Read verse 12 again

Human experience teaches us that frustrated expectations may cause a loss of morale and a sense of hopelessness. This proverb isn't promising instant gratification of all our wants, but that it's important to have right and realistic goals in life.

▷ *What goals do you have in life?*
▷ *Are they realistic?*
▷ *Do you think God approves of your goals?*
▷ *How do you handle it when your hopes are put on hold?*

MARK
True identity

65 – A TERRIFYING MAN
▷ *Who do the evil spirits recognise Jesus is? (v7)*

And they're right! They get Jesus' identity long before the disciples do! So why are they still "evil" spirits, if they know who Jesus is? Because they hate who He is. They don't want Jesus to be their Master. It's a reminder that what matters isn't just knowing who Jesus is, but loving who Jesus is, and treating Jesus as our God.

66 – HELP...
Does Jesus always heal people when they ask Him to?

Read 2 Corinthians 12 v 7–10
▷ *Why did Jesus give him a "thorn in [his] flesh"? (v7)*

▷ *Paul "pleaded" with Him to take this problem away, three times (v8). How did the Lord respond? (v9)*

And look how Paul responded! He was "delighted" to be weakened, so that everyone would realise that Jesus was working strongly through him (v10). His pain didn't make him angry or despairing; he knew Jesus had given it to him for a reason, and he got on with serving Him.

67 – DEAD SLEEPY
The people who knew this girl were crying and wailing in grief (v38).
Read 1 Thessalonians 4 v 13–17
Paul describes dead Christians as having "fallen asleep" (v15), because to Jesus, raising someone from the dead is like waking someone up.

▷ *Why do Christians not grieve like other people, "who have no hope"?*
▷ *How does v16–17 make you feel?*
▷ *What will you do about it? (v18)*

68 – HOMETOWN HERO?
Read Jeremiah 1 v 1 and 11 v 21–23
▷ *How was the prophet Jeremiah treated in his own hometown?*
▷ *How seriously did God take his treatment? (v22–23)*

We might not live in Anathoth, or Nazareth. But we are humans who live in a world which rejects the God-man Jesus. We deserve God's punishment too. Thank Jesus that He Himself takes the punishment that we deserve for not honouring Him properly.

121

69 – WORKING FOR THE KING

▶ **Read Mark 10 v 45; 1 Peter 3 v 18;
2 Corinthians 5 v 21**

▶ *Choose one of these verses, and
practise using it to explain the
message of Christianity.*

▶ *Then memorise that verse, so
you're ready to do your job!*

70 – DO THE RIGHT THING

Read Luke 23 v 8–12

Jesus has been arrested and is on trial.
And Herod's so pleased to meet Him —
he's been hoping to for a while (v8).

▶ *Why? (v8)*

▶ *How does Jesus respond? (v9)*

It's as though it's too late for Herod by this
stage. He'd hardened His heart and done
the easy thing rather than the right one —
now the only person who can forgive him
doesn't speak to him. And Herod doesn't
do the right thing and beg for mercy, but
does the easy thing, mocking Him (v11).
Tragic. And stupid.

71 – FOOD FOR THOUGHT

Jesus tells the disciples to feed the crowd
(v37). And they can't, of course!

▶ *But what do they end up doing?
(v41, middle sentence)*

In a way, they end up doing exactly what
Jesus told them to do! But they can only
do it because Jesus gives the food to them
to pass on. Effective Christians don't think
they can help others by themselves, based
on their own abilities. But they do know

that they can give to others what Jesus
has given to them.

▶ *Who could you love today / be
generous to / speak kindly to / look
out for / tell about eternal life?*

72 – LAKEWALK

Re-read verses 51–52

▶ *How do the disciples respond? (v51)*
(Remember, this means "confused".)

▶ *What else haven't they got their
heads round? (v52)*

Mark tells us this is because their "hearts
were hardened". They simply can't
understand who Jesus is. It will need God
to work in them to enable them to get it.

Can you grasp the truth that Jesus is God?
If you're struggling with it, ask God to
help your heart to get it. Are you trying to
tell others that Jesus is God? Make sure
you ask God to work in their hearts.

73 – ACTING STUPID

The Pharisees looked down on the
disciples for not keeping some rules (v1–2)
while they themselves were completely
ignoring some of God's rules (v9–12).

▶ *Are there things about other people
that make you look down on them,
even though God doesn't care about
those things?*

Read Exodus 20 v 3–17

▶ *Are there any commandments you
ignore because they're inconvenient
for how you want to live?*

74 – INSIDE OUT OR OUTSIDE IN?
Read Galatians 5 v 22–25

God's Spirit lives in Christians to change their hearts. He doesn't just get rid of sinful rubbish; He grows His fruit in us, too. Which parts of the fruit of the Spirit do you need to pray for some of, or more of? Ask for them now!

75 – CRUMBS OF COMFORT
Mark's Gospel is full of surprising people who have real faith…

Read 1 v 14–17; 10 v 46–52; 14 v 3–9; 15 v 39

And surprising people who don't get it at all…

Read 3 v 6; 10 v 17-22; 14 v 10-11

It's a reminder that Christians aren't amazing people (quite the opposite). It's Jesus who's amazing. His people don't love themselves or rely on themselves, but on Him — because He's much greater than we are!

76 – HOW TO SPOT GOD IN A CROWD
Read Mark 10 v 46–52

▶ *How is this four down, none to go?*
The conclusion is easy: Here is God in human flesh! If you're a Christian, this should encourage you — you're not an idiot for believing Jesus is God's Son. In fact you're simply following the evidence. And it should excite you… you are friends with the God of the universe!

77 – COOKERY CLASS
God fed His people with miraculous bread, or "manna" in the desert.

Read Deuteronomy 8 v 3

▶ *What was this meant to teach them?*
We're not sitting with Jesus and 4000 others in a remote place. But we do need feeding by Him. We need spiritual food — to be full up with "every word that comes from the mouth of the LORD". We need to be reading, remembering and loving God's words in the Bible. Reading Engage regularly is a great way to do that!

78 –THE WHOLE PICTURE?
Jesus asks His questions "around Caesarea Philippi" (v27). This was a place built to honour the Roman Emperor, or Caesar; a man who was treated as a god. It was also famous for its worship of Pan, a "god" who was thought to have the form of a human.

And it's here that Peter begins to realise that Jesus is the real God come to earth as a man. Casearea Philippi stood for wrong ideas about God-men; it's now gone down in history as the place where the God-man was recognised. Cool, eh?

79 – TELLING JESUS OFF
Re-read Mark 8 v 33

▶ *Jesus doesn't call Peter "Peter". What does He call him instead?*
When someone looks at the world from a perspective that isn't God's, they are being influenced by the devil. The devil is using Peter here to tempt Jesus to be a worldly, victorious king, instead of a suffering, dying Christ. It's a reminder that we need to see things from Jesus' point of view,

not the world's. And it's a reminder that we can be tempted to do wrong even by our closest Christian friends.

80 – HOW TO FOLLOW THE KING

Verse 34 is really helpful for reflecting on your day. As you go to bed each night, ask yourself these questions:

▶ *How have I denied what was easiest for me today?*

▶ *How have I died to the sinful things I wanted to do?*

▶ *How have I lived differently simply because I'm a follower of Jesus?*

Then you can praise Jesus for helping you to carry your cross. And, in the areas you've failed to, you can thank Him for dying on a cross to forgive you. And you can ask Him to help you be a better follower the next day.

81 – ASHAMED?

Read Mark 9 v 1

▶ *What would some people listening to Him see before they die?*

▶ *(Without looking down the page!) What do you think this means?*

It's unclear exactly when Jesus is talking about! It could be His transfiguration (v2–8), where some of the disciples see Jesus in all His heavenly glory. It could be His death, when Jesus opens the way into His kingdom. Or His resurrection, when He's raised to eternal life as King. Or the coming of His Spirit and the spreading of the kingdom message. Bible experts

disagree about exactly what Jesus meant. But the key thing is this: living in the 21st century, we know the kingdom of God has come with power. The risen King Jesus has opened the way into it, and His Spirit is at work, bringing people in.

PROVERBS

82 – WALKING GOD'S WAY

Read 1 Corinthians 1 v 26–31

Paul says his readers were not wise or influential, just ordinary. Like us. Yet God had chosen them to be wise.

▶ *How were they to become wise?*

▶ *What does Paul say true wisdom is? (v30)*

Now read Proverbs 13 all the way through, writing down all the words that refer to "wisdom", "the wise" or "the righteous".

▶ *If Christ is our wisdom and righteousness, how does that help us understand these verses better?*

▶ *If you replace "wisdom" and "the wise" etc with "Christ", what happens?*

83 – KICK OFF TIME

Read verse 4

Eh?? It's not entirely obvious what this proverb means. It might be saying no ox means no mess. But no oxen also means no ploughing, so no food. So maybe it's saying that no investment means no profit.

Read verse 10

Communication with others is important

and we must work hard to make sure we honour God in our conversations. But sometimes there are feelings that just can't be communicated.

Read verse 12

We can't always rely on instinct or feelings to guide us. Sometimes what seems like the right thing to do may not be right at all. Especially if it's a decision not based on true, godly wisdom.

84 – CASH AND CHARACTER

Read verse 27

One way the Bible defines wisdom is "the fear of the Lord" — showing respect for God and living His way. That's truly wise living. Turning away from sin and turning to God leads to true, eternal life. And it keeps us away from eternal death and sin's traps.

85 – WORD OF MOUTH

Read James 3 v 3–12

The tongue's often the last thing to be brought in line with Christian behaviour. Think what James would have to say to the "fools" described in the proverbs you've just read.

▶ *What would James say to you?*

87 – THE MASTER'S MASTERPLAN

Read Proverbs 16 v 10–15

The king mentioned here is God's chosen king for Israel. When he spoke, he spoke on God's behalf so it was important that... he was honest and fair (v10); he lived a right life for God (v12); that he punished

sin fairly and showed forgiveness (v14); he showed favour and mercy to his people (v15). Of course, no human king could always be perfect like this. Only the Christ — God's perfect, chosen King — rules without sin.

88 – FINAL WORDS OF WISDOM

**Read verse 16 again
and then Matthew 6 v 19–24
and 1 Timothy 6 v 17–19**

People who have a comfortable life (that includes most of us) can become arrogant. They trust in their own abilities and their money to get them through life. Paul says: *"Don't be so dumb — you can't put your trust in such uncertain things. Take your eyes off them and focus on trusting in and living for God. Then you'll really enjoy all He's given you."*

If God has given you stuff, be generous and give to others. We shouldn't be looking to grab what we can in this life. We must serve God with what we've got, be generous, and wait for the rewards and perfect life of eternity with God.

89 –HAIRY STUFF

**Read Exodus 29 v 1–9
and then 1 Peter 2 v 5 and 9**

All true believers are ordained ministers! They are washed in Jesus' blood, clothed in His righteousness and anointed by the Holy Spirit to equip them to serve Him in the world. Together we are God's priests, "ordained" to bring God to the world and the world to God.

engage wants to hear from YOU!

ⓘ Share experiences of God at work in your life
ⓘ Any questions you have about the Bible or the Christian life?
ⓘ How can we make *engage* better?

Email us — **martin@thegoodbook.co.uk**

Or send us a letter/postcard/cartoon/cheesecake to: engage, Blenheim House, 1 Blenheim Road, Epsom, Surrey, KT19 9AP, UK

In the next **engage**

Nehemiah Back in business
Mark On the road with Jesus
1 Chronicles Walk this way
2 & 3 John Sure sign
Proverbs Living for God
Plus: Eternal life
Why go to church?
Serious Bible study
Toolbox & Real Lives

Order **engage** now!

Make sure you order the next issue of **engage**. Or even better, grab a one-year subscription to make sure **engage** lands in your hands as soon as it's out.

Call us to order in the UK on 0333 123 0880
International: +44 (0) 20 8942 0880

or visit your friendly neighbourhood website:
UK: www.thegoodbook.co.uk
N America: www.thegoodbook.com
Australia: www.thegoodbook.com.au
New Zealand: www.thegoodbook.co.nz